HIDDEN HISTORY
of
HENRY COUNTY, INDIANA

HIDDEN HISTORY
of
HENRY COUNTY, INDIANA

Darrel Radford

THE
History
PRESS

Published by The History Press
Charleston, SC
www.historypress.com

First published 2024

Manufactured in the United States

ISBN 9781467156707

Library of Congress Control Number: 2024931457

To Cheryl Radford May, my dear sister who died before this book was published; Doug Magers, who opened the door for my historical journeys forty years ago, and to Becky Smith Radford, the best parts of my past, present and future.

CONTENTS

Introduction   9

Black History   11
Business   35
Disease   57
Memorable Faces and Places   75
Military   101
Politics   139
Sports   147
Unforgettable Events   173

About the Author   189

INTRODUCTION

Henry County, Indiana, has some of the most fertile farmland in the state. Underneath the sod, where corn and soybeans grow in abundance, is another "bumper crop," one of historic proportions. You can find it in the county seat of New Castle, which produced two battle-tested generals and nationally recognized basketball stars, as well as the tiny town of Mooreland, where a man almost became Indiana governor. "World's largest and finest" are words that spring up from deep, historic roots. Like roses once famous here, they bloom in brilliant color, only to fade with the passage of time. But they are still there for those who look.

This book explores the many historic links, people and places that make Henry County, Indiana, a most unique place. Author Darrel Radford, a lifelong resident of the county who grew up in Mooreland, wrote a regular newspaper column for the *Courier-Times* over a ten-year period from 2014 through 2023. These columns are reprinted in this book with permission of Paxton Media Group, parent company of the New Castle newspaper, which is the eighth oldest in Indiana.

So hop aboard a Maxwell automobile and take a journey back in time. From the melodic sounds of a Jesse French piano to the organized compartments of an authentic Hoosier Kitchen Cabinet, discover the hidden history that blends in with the beautiful landscape here. History is waiting to be uncovered.

BLACK HISTORY

COMING TO THE AID OF FREDERICK DOUGLASS

It is not light that we need, but fire; it is not the gentle shower, but thunder.
We need the storm, the whirlwind, and the earthquake.
—Frederick Douglass

The year was 1843. Henry County, Indiana, was just a few decades old. A new courthouse was less than a decade old when a man seeking justice for his people came through this area with a voice like thunder, an energy like a whirlwind and a cause like an earthquake.

Former Maryland slave Frederick Douglass, described by Spiceland resident and Earlham history professor Dr. Thomas Hamm as "one of the most important figures in 19th century American history," found refuge in the small Henry County community of Greensboro after escaping a mob attack in Pendleton.

Extensive research by Dr. Hamm, articles written by late Henry County historian Herbert Heller and an editorial published a few years ago in the *Anderson Herald Bulletin* allow us to share the deep historic rumblings that essentially occurred right in Henry County's own backyard.

The *Herald Bulletin* explained in its editorial that the New England Anti-Slavery Society sent orators around the country to make one hundred speeches promoting abolition in 1843. That's why Douglass came to deliver a speech not far from the banks of Fall Creek in Pendleton.

Above: This National Park Service image shows a young Frederick Douglass. He would have been about twenty-five years old when visiting Henry County, Indiana, in 1843. *National Park Service.*

Opposite: Dr. Tom Hamm, a Spiceland resident, is among the world's leading experts on Quakers in America. He taught history for thirty-six years at Earlham College. *Tom Hamm.*

As the Anderson newspaper reported, according to Tom McClintock of the Pendleton Historical Museum, a group of men attacked the speakers with clubs and eggs as the speeches began. Had it not been for a few sympathetic people at the event, Douglass might have been killed. He suffered an arm injury that historians say never healed, but he survived the attack.

A short time later, Seth Hinshaw, a well-known Quaker active in Underground Railroad activities, gave Douglass refuge at Greensboro, a small town west of New Castle. The great freedom fighter and orator is said to have given a speech in Greensboro's Liberty Hall before he left. "Greensboro was about as safe a place as you could find in 1843, since it was so strongly anti-slavery," Dr. Hamm said.

Hinshaw may not have known it then, but he was aiding what history tells us was a remarkable man, someone born into slavery who grew up to defy a ban on teaching slaves to read and write, ultimately becoming one of the most eloquent statesmen of his time.

But then, Hinshaw himself was described by Dr. Hamm as perhaps "the most unusual and most fascinating person ever to live in Henry County…a brooding, bearded figure with the countenance of an Old Testament prophet." His sheltering of Douglass was just one of many things Hinshaw did to promote the abolitionist cause. He ran a "free produce" store in Greensboro, meaning none of his goods had any connection to slave labor; he led a campaign to desegregate the town's school; and he hosted numerous meetings of reformers.

Dr. Hamm said it appears that Douglass was probably in Henry County no more than "a day or two" before heading east to Wayne County and then into Ohio. But he says it is "very likely" that Douglass delivered a speech in Greensboro before he left.

While Indiana is generally regarded as a state that opposed slavery, some may not realize how divided Hoosiers were on the issue, making it even more courageous for Hinshaw to take the actions he did regarding Douglass and other abolitionists.

"Abolitionists were very unpopular with a lot of northerners," Dr. Hamm said. "There are a lot of complicated reasons for that. There was a fear that black people, if given equality, would compete with white men for jobs and perhaps threaten white women."

 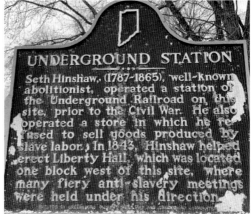

Left: Seth Hinshaw was a devout Quaker from Greensboro, a small town west of New Castle, who helped Frederick Douglass after he was attacked in Pendleton. *Henry County Historical Society*.

Right: This marker remains in Greensboro, population 123. Here Quaker Seth Hinshaw ran a "free produce" store with no items for sale created by slave labor. *Henry County Historical Society*.

Hamm said that Henry County was somewhat split on the issue, with antislavery forces generally stronger in the southern part of the county. "It was probably more than anything else, the Quaker influence," Hamm said. Meanwhile Prairie, Jefferson and Fall Creek Townships "had a lot of settlers who were anti-abolitionists," Hamm added. "Abolitionists were seen by some as fanatics who threatened to break up the United States."

The final words of the 2012 Anderson editorial also seem to apply here in Henry County regarding historical markers: "Such signposts remind local residents of the power of their own history."

FREDERICK DOUGLASS SPEAKS AT HENRY COUNTY COURTHOUSE

More than a decade had passed since the end of the Civil War, but on a Friday night in the early fall of 1876, a packed crowd in the Henry County Courthouse learned that the struggle for Black people continued. They heard it from one of the most powerful antislavery voices of the nineteenth century: Frederick Douglass. The former slave who first came to Henry County in 1843 and was given refuge by Greensboro's Seth Hinshaw was back, this time as a free man. The *New Castle Courier* reported the event this way in its September 29, 1876 edition:

> *The speech of Fred Douglass at the court house on Tuesday night was an important event in the campaign in Henry county. Although the meeting was little advertised, the court house was densely crowded, and the close attention manifested, showed the respect entertained for the distinguished orator. The audience, too, was different from the audiences found at ordinary political meetings. The old anti-slavery pioneers were out in force to hear the man whose utterances had been so potent in creating an anti-slavery sentiment in the north.*
>
> *It was Mr. Douglass' second appearance at New Castle. In the summer of 1843 he spoke at the old court house in this place and those who heard the speech remember that he recounted upon that occasion the story of the brutal outrage which was committed upon him at Pendleton a few days before by Democrats of Madison county. The changes which have occurred in the nation since that time seem marvelous. Then slavery existed in one-half of the Union. The Fugitive Slave law was upon the statute books, Negroes were forbidden by law to come into the state of Indiana, and John Tyler was in the Presidential chair. When Mr. Douglass traveled through*

Frederick Douglass spoke at this New Castle courthouse in 1843 while traveling through east-central Indiana. *Henry County Historical Society.*

This is what the Henry County Courthouse would have looked like when Frederick Douglass spoke in New Castle as a free man in 1876. *Henry County Historical Society.*

the North, he was subject to outrage and insult, while he would have been remanded to slavery if he had visited the South.

Upon the occasion of Mr. Douglass' second appearance at New Castle, he came as an enfranchised citizen, but he is still the earnest advocate of his race, whose wrongs, he believes, are to-day but little less than in many sections of the South than those endured thirty years ago. When Mr. Douglass appeared before the large audience, he was greeted with hearty

*applause. He is now about seventy-five years of age and his abundant hair
is nearly white. He is still vigorous and eloquent, but has lost some of the
fire of his youth; but when recounting the wrongs inflicted upon his people
by the Kuklux and White Leaguers of the South, his old fire seemed to
come back.*

While the newspaper article reported that there was passion in his voice,
pessimism also colored his tone and a sense of renewed urgency rose in
his words.

"Mr. Douglass regards the future of the country as dark, in the event
that the Democratic Party obtains control of the government," the *Courier*
article noted. "He is no alarmist; and spoke of a change of administrations
as being desirable in ordinary times, but the utter disregard for law in many
of the Southern States, the massacres at Coushatta and Hamburg and the
many thousands of murders of negroes by the Democrats of the South
filled him with forebodings for the future of his race. The people of the
North could scarcely comprehend the atrocity of the Southern Democrats,
and it was creditable to their civilization that they could not."

The Coushatta massacre in 1874, just two years prior to Douglass's
second appearance here, was an attack by members of a white supremacist
organization composed of white Southern Democrats, Republican
officeholders and freedmen in Coushatta, the parish seat of Red River
Parish, Louisiana. They assassinated six white Republicans and five to
twenty freedmen who were witnesses.

The Hamburg Massacre (or Red Shirt Massacre or Hamburg riot) was a
riot in the town of Hamburg, South Carolina, in July 1876, leading up to
the last election season of the Reconstruction era. It was the first in a series
of civil disturbances planned and carried out by white Democrats in the
majority-Black Republican Edgefield District, with the goal of suppressing
Black Americans' civil rights and voting rights.

The *Courier* article said that Douglass used both of these sad events as an
example that while the Civil War was over, civil injustices were not:

*Mr. Douglass adjured the people of the North to save, for the sake of
freedmen or the South, the government from falling into the hands of men
who, by reason of slavery, had so little regard for the welfare of colored
people of the nation. Questions of finance and tariff were of minor
importance compared with the existence of the nation and the supremacy of
law. As the sleeping babe is safest in the arms of its mother, so the freedom*

vouchsafed the nation by the Republican Party is safest when that party is in power. The address throughout was eloquent and philosophical, and showed a thorough knowledge of the animus and purposes of the late slave power of the South.

Douglass was as critical of Republicans, however, as he was Democrats in his speech here:

The Republican party had given them their freedom, but still owed a debt to them. It had emancipated them, but they were still without homes, without the means of gaining a livelihood and at the mercy of their offended masters. The Republican Party had given the Negro his freedom and it was now the duty of the party to protect him. The Democracy, by their policy of murdering the inoffensive and long suffering black men were to bring about a solid South for the Democratic party. But let them have a care. By their course, they bring about a solid north against them.…The Negro, when called upon to aid the Union, had rallied two hundred thousand strong. The Democratic Party had in times past been the defender of a hellish crime, which for gold sold human flesh on the auction block and sold babies to build churches. Even the pulpit had been the defender of slavery, and the minister was paid from the proceeds of human chattels. The speaker closed by saying the peace of the country depended upon the continued success of the Republican Party, and he believed it would succeed. The people of Indiana had a great duty to perform, and that was a vote for Harrison and Hayes.

The 1876 election saw the highest voter turnout of any in U.S. history (82 percent) and was decided by a single electoral vote. Rutherford B. Hayes was the eventual winner, and true to Douglass's wishes, Henry County supported him. Hayes received 65 percent of the vote here, winning over Democrat Samuel Tilden 3,631 to 1,924.

But Douglass would certainly have been disappointed in the Hayes administration. An article on the University of Virginia website by Sheila Black said that Hayes was unable to advance the cause of civil rights:

While Hayes strongly supported African Americans' right to vote and protection of their civil rights, he had little influence in the South. By the time he took office, the only federal troops still in the South protecting Republican governments were limited to small areas surrounding state houses in the capitals of New Orleans and Columbia. Hayes insisted that Democrats in

South Carolina and Louisiana pledged to uphold the civil and voting rights of black and white Republicans. Once the Democrats agreed, Hayes pulled the remaining federal troops out of the South. And white southerners quickly turned their backs on their pledges, systematically disenfranchising black voters through poll taxes, literacy tests, and intimidation. Democrats in the South created a segregated society that used terror and violence to oppress African Americans.

He [Hayes] bitterly complained in his diary, for example, about the fraud, intimidation, and "violence of the most atrocious character" that white southerners used to win elections in 1878. And he used his presidential veto multiple times to try to preserve some element of federal oversight over African American voting. But his efforts did little, and white supremacy dominated life in the southern states well into the second half of the 20th century.

STORY OF WILLIAM TRAIL SR. IS MICROCOSM OF BLACK STRUGGLE FOR FREEDOM

He was born a slave in Maryland. He was beaten and sold. He died a free man in Henry County, Indiana. The story in between of William Trail is remarkable, a microcosm of so many struggles Black people endured before, during and after the Civil War. It is a story of hard work daring danger in the face, all for the sake of freedom. The family raised as a result went on to do great things.

Historian Herbert Heller wrote that Trail escaped from a southern master in Maryland to become free man in Henry County, Indiana. The dramatic story was published in the *Indianian Magazine* in 1899. Written by Trail's eldest son, William, the paper was actually read before the Henry County Historical Society at its annual meeting that year. Heller reports that it was William Trail Jr. himself who read the story at that historical society meeting. Following are some excerpts from that story.

William Trail Sr. was born a slave on May 23, 1774, in Montgomery County, Maryland. Basil and Barbary Trail were said to be "his lawful owners."

"He never complained of ill treatment from the hands of his master during the days of his childhood," Trail Jr. wrote. "But the mistress took a dislike to him and made him the object of which to vent the fury of a very bad temper. She would beat him so he would run away and hide until almost starved, and the master would become uneasy about his property and search the premises until he found him."

Left: From the Henry County Historical Society archives, this photo of William Trail shows him in his later years. He endured many hardships before finding the best years of his life in Henry County. *Henry County Historical Society*.

Right: Dr. Herbert Heller chronicled William Trail's story in a three-volume *Historic Henry County* series in the early 1980s that's still a go-to reference today. *From the* Courier-Times.

At the age of twelve, William was sold for $300 to James Blakely, a farmer in Lawrence County, South Carolina. It was here that the real dreams of freedom took root.

"Will worked away on the farm, of which he in time became almost manager, going with his master once a year and sometimes oftener wagoning or rolling tobacco to Charleston," Trail Jr. wrote. "On a few occasions he went to Savannah and Augusta, Ga. As Will grew up, he became strongly impressed with the fact that he was a man and entitled to the proceeds of his own labor. He saw that on him depended the success of the family and for his services, he was very poorly fed and clad."

"At last he dared to tell the old man that he had a right to better clothes, but the master could not see it just that way," Trail Jr. continued. "But Will would not give up. He then proposed to work for the master five days of the week and have one for himself and furnish all of his clothes."

So the first real contract of his life was now in place for William Trail Sr. In time, he bought a colt from one of the master's sons. But the contract was both a blessing and a curse. "He was treated kindly by all of the family except the old master and one of the boys," Trail Jr. wrote. "He valued Will highly as property but he became jealous and abusive because he thought that his slave was doing too well and thought too much of himself."

"The slave was now ruined as property," Trail Jr. continued. "Will was a man up in his twenties, and the one day of freedom in each week had done its work. Having once tasted the sweet morsel of liberty, there was no more contentment as a slave."

The Underground Railroad, that glorious secret network for helping slaves escape from the South to the North and Canada in the years before the Civil War, had not yet been developed. But a yearning for freedom had lodged itself in William Trail Sr.'s heart.

"Will was near 30 years old, and thought himself the possessor of a horse and saddle, saddlebags, pretty good clothes and some money," Trail Jr. wrote. "So he thought the next thing most needful for him was to possess his own body."

There was a full moon on a Thursday night in August when William Trail Sr. gathered the few earthly possessions he had worked so hard to obtain. He mounted his horse and headed to what was then known as the Indiana Territory. Trail carried with him a piece of paper written for him by one of the master's sons who did not approve of how he had been treated. The paper said simply, "Let William Trail pass and repass as a freeman and disturb him not."

He was on his way. But the trials and tribulations of the slavery he so desperately wanted to leave behind would follow him.

Trials and Tribulations Followed William Trail Sr.

"Is that a free man with you?" The question came more than once as a solitary Black man accompanied two friendly white men on the road to Indiana. It was the fall of 1814, a time when the leaves on the trees—and the hearts of men—were about to show their true colors.

The two white men answered in affirmative tones each time the question was asked. "We think he is," they answered. "He pays his own way and takes his turn with us filling the bottle."

The trials and tribulations of that lone Black man—William Trail Sr.—are chronicled in the book *Historic Henry County* by Herbert Heller. Heller wrote that Trail's escape from a southern master in Maryland to become a free man in Henry County, Indiana, was published in the *Indianian Magazine* in 1899. Written by Trail's eldest son, William Jr., the magazine article was actually read aloud by him to members of the Henry County Historical Society at its annual meeting that year.

A modern-day Indiana Historical Society magazine, *Traces*, also profiled the trials and tribulations of Trail in its winter 2013 edition. It is a story of many twists and turns on one man's long and winding road to freedom. It is also a story with a Henry County ending. The final resting place of the Trail family is located a half mile east of Shirley.

Trail's story takes a literal turn for the worst after the kind-hearted men who affirmed him a "free man" stopped at a home where some of their relatives lived. They invited Trail to join them there for a few days. But Trail excused himself, saying that his money was growing short and he would rather be journeying onward. In retrospect, it was a decision that made his quest for freedom so much harder.

Now alone, Trail reached Lexington, Kentucky, where citizens were not so kind. They objected to his proceeding farther and took him before a justice of the peace. "The justice told them that he did not have the law and could not dispose of the case," Trail Jr. wrote. "They took him to another justice and he asked him where he was from, what county, the name of the clerk of the court and all the officers, all of which he answered satisfactorily."

"Then he proceeded to examine his pass," Trail Jr. continued. "It was done up in a minute of the Baptist Association."

The judge pronounced it worthless and hung his head in meditation. But then he said, "I will have nothing to do with him." William Trail Sr. was released. When he was ferried across the Ohio River—then the dividing line between slave states and free states—he had "a lighter heart than he had done for many days." But laws and the hearts of men are two very different things.

Long before twenty-four-hour cable television news and the internet, news still found a way to travel, particularly when it involved the former "property" of a slave owner.

"Word was promptly sent back to the old master, who was not the man to give up so valuable a property without an effort to reclaim the same," Trail Jr. wrote. "The old man [James Blakely] saddled his horse and followed on to Indiana. Not thinking it wise to tackle his slave personally, he stopped…

and employed a man named Harvey to go and arrest Will…and bring him to Brookville."

Blakely's agent lied in the name of compassion to capture Trail. He found him hard at work cutting on a log as part of a road crew and offered to take over and give Trail a few minutes of rest. When William gladly accepted the offer and handed over his axe, the agent took hold of Trail "and commanded all in the name of the State" to assist him.

"They gathered around him so he saw resistance was useless," Trail Jr. wrote. "He was tied and put on a horse with his feet tied under…and away they started for Brookville."

Trail was tied so he could only use his arms from the elbows out. "He commenced trying to untie the rope which was tied behind his back," Trail Jr. wrote. "The man looking back asked what he was doing. He moved away his hands and said 'Nothing.'"

Then the story took a dramatic turn. Harvey took hold of the rope and jerked Trail so as to raise his anger, and he commenced to boldly untie himself. William Trail escaped capture. He ultimately lost all of his earthly belongings but gained something priceless: his freedom.

"You have taken me thus unaware, but after this you nor any other man will ever take me alive," Trail said as he left his captor. "And you may tell Blakely that he may sell me or do as he pleases, but I will not serve him another day."

Trail's hard work paid off. "That force of character which had carried him thus far was destined to bear him through," Trail Jr. said. "He went to work clearing the land, always preferring to take jobs and be his own boss. He claimed the honor of having cleared the timber off the first lot in the town of Brownsville in Union County."

William Trail Sr. was free at last. Henry County was his destiny. But more trouble lay ahead.

"These Truths" Not So Self-Evident for William Trail Sr.

"We hold these truths to be self-evident, that all men are created equal, that they are endowed by their Creator with certain unalienable rights, that among these are Life, Liberty and the Pursuit of happiness." On July 4, 1833, a mere fifty-seven years after the founding fathers signed the Declaration of Independence featuring those words, one Black man destined to live in Greensboro Township, Henry County, Indiana, was still risking his life for liberty. Despite those "self-evident" truths, he remained the one being pursued.

William Trail Sr., who had escaped from a southern landowner in Maryland, no longer lived in a slave state. But worry was still his master.

Late Henry County historian Herbert Heller wrote that Trail had moved his family to the western part of Greensboro Township from Fayette County that year. The man he left behind, however, was not so keen to give up on what he considered "his property." And before he would find friendlier faces in Greensboro Township, Trail had to endure not only more tribulations but also the prospect of an actual trial.

The story was told by Trail's eldest son, William Jr., at the Henry County Historical Society's 1899 annual meeting. Even though he had no idea where Trail had gone, James Blakely, the former slave owner, was able to "trade" him to a man named John Cleveland for a horse. After the transaction, Cleveland was hot on the trail for Trail.

"He found a man at what was called the north bend of the Ohio River named Sam Hedge, who kept a ferry and a made a business of getting slaves across and directing them where to go. When they [their former masters] came and offered a reward, he would bring the slaves in and receive the reward," Heller's account read. "So John Cleveland, the trader, employed Sam Hedge, the slave catcher, to catch and bring back William Trail, the freeman, to be enslaved again."

"At that time, he [Trail] was making his home near Connersville," Heller's book stated. "The kidnapping party came up to Connersville and by bribery or some other means secured the services of the sheriff of Fayette County to assist in their unlawful business. They came for him one cold winter day and found him helping a neighbor to butcher hogs."

Trail was informed that "he was wanted to answer to a civil writ in a case of debt." When he asked to whom, the sheriff "looked at his papers and said to John Cleveland."

Obviously, Trail had no idea who John Cleveland was. He thought himself a free man, but had been traded for like a piece of property. Ultimately, after deception by the men who found him, Trail was jailed to stand trial.

Justice was done not by the court, but rather by concerned Fayette County residents. "All arrived at Connersville and Trail pleaded not ready for trial and was given three days' time and lodged in jail," Heller's book noted. "The circumstances created great excitement among the people of the surrounding neighborhood. They visited him at the jail, first one, then another, so he had company most of the time."

"Finally the people concluded that the kidnappers having the sheriff on their side, would steal the prisoner away on the night before the day set for trial," continued Heller's book. "To provide against such a contingency, the people gathered in town, armed with other available means of defense. They hauled in logs and built a great fire in front of the jail and stood guard all night, the weather being very cold."

"The kidnapping party saw the hopelessness of their plans and sat around in despair at the hotel until a late hour in the night, then called for their horses and made way for the Ohio River," Heller's book stated. "On the next day when the trial was called, nobody appeared against Trail and he was released."

It was the last time an attempt was made to enslave William Trail Sr. The pursuit was now all his, and happiness was the target.

A growing Trail family sold their Fayette County land in 1832 and entered 160 acres of land located on the west part of Greensboro Township in Henry County. The former slave raised a family full of soldiers. Four of Trail's seven sons enlisted in the forces of the Union army in the Civil War. Three died in service, fighting for the same cause Revolutionary War soldiers had fought for less than a century before.

In 1831, two years before William Trail Sr. brought his family to Henry County, the words "Let freedom ring" were first penned by Samuel Francis Smith in the song "My Country 'Tis of Thee." The seminary student's prose became one of America's de facto national anthems.

Trail was one of many Black citizens who had to work extra hard for that freedom "in the land where my fathers died." He had to work extra hard to show, by example, that all lives matter in the land of the pilgrims' pride—that freedom should ring for Americans of every color "from every mountainside."

He desperately wanted to be included in the pronoun of the song title. *My country 'tis of thee.*

Early Black Family Buried Near Shirley Found Peace, Prosperity in Henry County

After years of struggle, abuse, escape efforts and legal challenges, William Trail Sr., the former slave, found peace and tranquility at last in Henry County. So wrote late historian Herbert Heller in his three-volume *Historic Henry County* set.

William Trail's grave site was surrounded by weeds, but an effort led by Donna Tauber of the Henry County Cemetery Commission cleaned up the cemetery. *Donna Tauber*.

"He spent the last ten years of his life in comparative peace and quietude," Heller's book stated. "One of the greatest desires of his age was to live to see all men free."

That wish did not come true for him, as Trail died at his Henry County home on September 16, 1858, at the age of seventy-five. But some members of his family did taste the sweetness of freedom and made the most of it.

The *Courier-Times*, through Heller's writings and other state historic sources, tried to retell the Trail's family story. Today, the final resting place of the Trail family is located a half mile east of Shirley, a small town west of New Castle. The cemetery was overtaken by weeds and vegetation. Henry County Cemetery Commission president Donna Tauber brought the Trail family story to light and worked with the private landowner to have the cemetery cleared.

The Trail family's story was profiled not only in Heller's books, but also as part of biographical memoirs published in 1902 by the B.F. Bowen Company in Logansport, Indiana. The family were also featured in *Traces*, a state historical magazine. The memoirs and magazine shed even more light on a family history that's fascinating as well as uplifting—and, in some cases, tragic.

The Trails Grove Cemetery, the final resting place of the William Trail family, is located near the small town of Shirley, just a few miles west of New Castle. *Donna Tauber.*

William Trail Sr.'s sons offered their services and lives, if necessary, in defense of their country. William Jr. enlisted in 1865 "and gallantly performed his part in that awful strife," the memoirs read. William Jr. was one of four brothers who enlisted in the Union forces. Three—James, David and Benjamin—died fighting for freedom.

The Trail family members weren't looking for handouts. They worked hard to reach for the American dream. The memoirs state that William Trail Jr. used a small government pension and a large amount of hard work to pay for 160 acres, worth about $9,000 at the time.

"All of this has been gained as a result of his own earnest and unremitting efforts and Mr. Trail certainly deserves great credit for what he accomplished," the biographical memoirs stated.

Patriotic and energetic, state sources indicate that Trail was steadfast in trying to better himself. "Mr. Trail keeps alive his old army associations by membership in Post No. 360 G.A.R. at Spiceland. In his political affiliations he was a Republican up to the election of 1896, since which time he has supported the Democratic party."

"He is a gentleman, who in all circumstances in which he has been placed has borne himself with that spirit which brings to a man the respect and esteem of the entire community. He has in all respects been the architect of his own fortunes and has [built] wisely and well," the memoirs concluded.

Heller concurred in his historical description of the family. "Both the son and father were successful farmers and the 1857 map of Henry County shows two farms in central and western Greensboro Township owned by William Trail."

Education was also a top priority for the family. "The school which the Trail children attended was the Union Literary Institute in Randolph County," Heller wrote. "After the Trail children had completed the course in this school, they returned to Henry County and here the eldest son, William, assisted by other brothers opened an elementary school for their younger brothers and other colored children of the neighborhood."

Yet before William Trail Sr. brought his family to Henry County, he had to take on the then unprecedented task of fighting an unfounded arson charge in a Fayette County court—a charge brought forth by James Smith, a Baptist minister. Here is an excerpt from the *Traces* magazine article published by the Indiana Historical Society in 2013:

> In *Early Indiana Trials and Sketches*, Oliver H. Smith related that one night about midnight (probably in 1827) James's large barn caught fire and burned to the ground. James openly charged Trail with arson. Trail responded by securing Oliver's services to pursue a slander suit.
>
> According to Oliver, there was "no evidence whatsoever of his guilt and very few believe the charge." The allegation of arson was evidently not pursued by the authorities.

But Trail's reputation was damaged, and he wanted his name restored. "It is a remarkable testament to the self-confidence and determination of a former slave that his slander case against a white defendant would be brought before an eastern Indiana court in the 1820s," the article's authors, Charles Hubbard and Georgia Cravey, wrote. "Even the remotest possibility that a favorable verdict for Trail would be forthcoming required an unprecedented faith in the law and judicial process."

Once barely visible, the Trails Grove Cemetery has been cleaned up, preserving the resting place of a Black family who made Henry County home. *Donna Tauber.*

The trial lasted three days. Ultimately, the court found in favor of Trail and awarded him a twenty-five-dollar settlement. "The size of the settlement was not as important to Trail as the restoration of his good name and the vindication of his faith in the judicial system," Hubbard and Cravey concluded.

Stories like these are why the Henry County Cemetery Commission members believed the Trail family cemetery should be cleaned up and restored as a genuine historic site. There are other compelling reasons as well. It's one of only two Black cemeteries in Henry County. Grandson Archibald Jr., nicknamed "Boss," was a noted painter and artist. "The business signs, many done in gold leaf in Shirley and Wilkinson, were almost exclusively his work," Tauber said. William Trail Sr.'s son Barzillai, also buried here, learned the carpenter's trade at an early age and made an extended trip to Canada, only to return here and become a successful farmer.

Leora Trail, one of three daughters born to Barzillai and Susan Fear Trail, left $5,408.63 to the renowned Tuskegee Institute in Alabama and charged the facility to "take care of and keep in a respectable condition at all times a certain burial lot known as 'Trail's Graveyard,' one-half mile east of the town of Shirley." However, there is no documentation that it received these funds. The mystery of what happened to those funds continues to elude Tauber. But she's determined to preserve the history that's here, an important Henry County footnote in America's continuing struggle for racial equality.

Spiceland Baseball Star Broke Racial Barriers Years before Jackie Robinson

John "Snowball" Merida had it all in terms of baseball skill. If he were alive today, Merida would fit into that coveted "five-tool" player category—meaning he could hit for average, hit for power, run the bases well, field his position and possess a strong throwing arm.

What Merida didn't have was the right skin color for the prejudicial times. He was Black, and he grew up in Spiceland, Indiana.

Merida was destined to become Henry County's Jackie Robinson before the man who broke baseball's color barrier was even born.

In the early 1900s, the Chicago Cubs had the brilliant infield trio known as "Tinker to Evers to Chance." While their skills turned 491 double plays in a four-year span, it was "Ratcliff to Hamm to Painter" that turned a light on Spiceland's Merida, perhaps the best player today's fans never saw.

Henry County historian Richard P. Ratcliff had a young man named Tom Hamm in his New Castle middle school class. Hamm went on to become a professor at Earlham College. Alex Painter was in one of Hamm's classes at the Richmond, Indiana school.

Because of Ratcliff and Hamm's influence, Painter was introduced to this forgotten phenom. The introduction became an obsession for Painter, who ended up authoring a book titled *Baseball Immortal: The Odyssey of Trailblazing Slugger John "Snowball" Merida.*

In the book, how and why the family came to Spiceland becomes crystal clear. Years before baseball would become a big part of his life, John Merida's mother was longing to be "safe at home." "Though predominantly rural and fairly small, with a population of just a few hundred in the 1870s, Spiceland had an African American community that predated even the conclusion of the American Civil War," Painter wrote.

In another paragraph, Painter stated, "Though Spiceland wasn't free of racial prejudice, it was considered 'light years ahead of their white neighbors.' In fact, one account from the 1880s states that Blacks from North Carolina regarded Spiceland as 'Jerusalem.'"

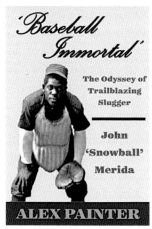

Top: Richard P. Ratcliff served as Henry County historian for forty years and authored many history-related books. *Richard Ratcliff.*

Bottom: Alex Painter authored this book about John "Snowball" Merida, a Spiceland baseball phenom in the early 1900s. *Alex Painter.*

It was Spiceland where a strong Quaker church congregation "fought slavery fervently," Painter wrote. It was Spiceland where the Underground Railroad led many Black slaves to safety, thanks in large part to a Greensboro man named Seth Hinshaw. And it was Hinshaw who helped renowned abolitionist Frederick Douglass, one of the most important figures in nineteenth-century history, find refuge in nearby Greensboro after a vicious attack in Pendleton.

So John "Snowball" Merida had landed in the right place, even if it was at the wrong time. While his ancestors were slaves, he was destined to become a household name on baseball fields from Spiceland and New Castle to Indianapolis and Cincinnati, even on to Kansas City.

"A half century before Jackie Robinson graced a major league baseball field, John Merida was an indomitable force of integration among the patchy meadows, dusty sandlots and ramshackle municipal parks, all situated among the unassuming cornfields of the Hoosier state," Painter wrote. "As a black man in the first decade of the 20th century, he'd ultimately reach the pinnacle of the sport that was available to him."

After starring for Spiceland Academy from 1895 to 1903, "Snowball" played on seven other teams over the next decade. Wherever he went, "Snowball" made life miserable for opposing pitchers. An Indianapolis newspaper writer described him this way: "He is the terror of all pitchers. His long hitting is attracting the attention of the Middle West and if he were a white man, he would be in the professional leagues."

One might say that John Merida's popularity "snowballed" every place he went. From Spiceland Academy to the Krell-French New Castle team and the Montpelier "Oil Boys," people from all parts of the Midwest flocked to see him hit a baseball.

His athletic prowess continued professionally for the Cincinnati Black Tourists and the Indianapolis ABCs. His personality and athletic ability also made headlines for the Minneapolis Keystones and the Kansas City Royal Giants.

Why was he nicknamed "Snowball"? Painter explained in his book: "Merida is incredibly affable and unwaveringly friendly. After every game at Spiceland Academy, he would get mobbed by all the fans (especially the children), regardless if they won or lost. It was because of his friendliness he garnered his more famous nickname—'Snowball.' After his time was over at the Academy, he played for local semi-pro teams all over east central Indiana, sometimes still being the only black player on the team. Merida got his big break in 1907, when he was signed by the Indianapolis ABCs."

In 108 games from 1907 to 1910 with the Indianapolis team, "Snowball" had a batting average of .313, hit nineteen home runs and earned a slugging percentage of .603. A slugging percentage is defined as the total number of bases a player records per at-bat.

Putting that into historical perspective, Major League Baseball's all-time slugging percentage leader is the legendary Babe Ruth. His career slugging percentage was .529. The more Painter learned about "Snowball," the deeper entrenched he became in this incredible story.

One could point to June 5, 1896, as the day "Snowball" started rolling. It was Spiceland Field Day, and the small southern Henry County town grew "by several hundred percent" to enjoy the multifaceted event. Appearing on the list of participants that day, according to Painter's research, was John Merida. "Given the demographics of Henry County, it is probable he was one of a handful, but possibly the only person of color competing in the contests," Painter wrote.

Merida toed the line in the one-hundred-yard dash. When the starting pistol sounded for the race to begin, it had all but ended. "With a blend of speed and grace, Merida, never taking his eyes off the finish line, crossed the ribbon in first place," Painter wrote. "He had left the entire pack of competitors in the dust."

The very next year, at the same event, Merida's speed took a back seat to his strength. "Every time the teenager swung the bat, the ball whistled through the air, alternating between blistering line drives and fly balls which cut across the Indiana sky in perfect arcs," Painter wrote. "Regardless of the launch angle, the ball continually traveled distances thought improbable by the thousands of dazzled spectators."

After Merida was crowned winner of the hitting contest, he was soon swarmed at home plate. "The men were giving him congratulatory back slaps and offering to buy him a concession from one of the vendors," Painter wrote. "Others had already beaten them to it, thrusting glass bottles of soda or cooked ears of corn in his direction. A throng of doting children, some of his biggest fans, clung to his cotton wool knickerbockers and followed his each and every step."

When the individual contest was over that day, Merida took his talents to the Spiceland Academy dugout and led his hometown team to a 23–12 pounding of county rival New Castle.

With Merida behind the plate as catcher, the Spiceland Academy rarely lost. Painter's research revealed that the Spiceland Academy team won more than 80 percent of its games when Merida was in the lineup.

Under the leadership of Richard Ratcliff, the Spiceland Alumni Association funded this marker for John "Snowball" Merida's grave. *Richard Ratcliff.*

Painter's discovery of Merida was like a *bloop* single with the bases loaded. "It was a total stumble-upon for me," Painter said. "I'm a Negro Leagues guy, and I did a history of Negro League baseball here in Richmond. I decided to see how many Negro League games were played in Richmond. I expected to find a handful, but I ended up finding 125. It was absolutely shocking.

"After I made this really nice registry of all these games, I thought, 'You know what would be really cool, Alex? If you could track every player who came to Richmond.' So then I started at the beginning of that list."

"This is just serendipity, but the very first game that took place in Richmond with a Negro League team was the 1907 Indianapolis ABCs," Painter continued. "The leadoff hitter for them was John Merida. He was playing second base. So I had no idea who he was. I went over to the Negro Leagues database. Then I said, 'My God, he's from Spiceland?'"

For Painter, who works as community engagement officer for the Wayne County Foundation in Richmond, it was like finding buried treasure. With Ratcliff and Hamm as resources, he began poring over Spiceland Friends Meeting minutes. He found images that Ratcliff had donated to the Indiana Historical Society. Painter and his son even visited Circle Grove Cemetery, where Merida is buried.

"So the very first player in that 350-player registry that I was creating for Richmond project—the very first player by virtue of batting leadoff in the very first game I found—was John Merida. I saw that not only was he from Spiceland, but he died less than four years after that game was played."

"I had never been to Spiceland before," said Painter, a Fort Wayne native. "My son, who was six at the time, and I walked all over the Circle Grove Cemetery trying to find his grave. He was incredibly obscure," Painter said. "His grave was unmarked for sixty-five years. The only reason it's marked to this day is Richard [Ratcliff], of course."

BUSINESS

EDWARDS JEWELERS:
A TRIED-AND-TRUE DOWNTOWN GLOW

Sparkling like a diamond, it shined through a great depression, a world war and even a pandemic. There have been multiple New Castle downtown comings and goings, Broad Street reconfigurations and reconstructions, yet it somehow endured. Through nineteen U.S. presidents (from Woodrow Wilson to Joe Biden), twenty-three Indiana governors (from James P. Goodrich to Eric Holcomb) and eighteen New Castle mayors (from J. Leb Watkins to Greg York), it remained a tried-and-true downtown jewel.

Edwards Jewelers turned one hundred years old in 2021, an amazing feat considering the economic ups and downs of the past century. While former neighbor Smith's is still operating on Indiana 3, Edwards was the lone downtown survivor in a long line of jewelry stores here dating back to 1873 until it finally closed in late 2023.

Alice Bowsman, just the third owner in that one-hundred-year period, smiled as she displayed the store's original retail merchant certificate dated January 3, 1921. Then, while holding a framed 100th anniversary certificate presented to her by the Indiana House of Representatives, her smile grew wider. "I made it—through a pandemic," Alice said.

When January 3, 2021, came, it marked fulfillment of a promise she made to Morris Edwards, whose father, H. Ray, started the business. "I always told him I would make it to 100th year," Alice said shortly after Morris died on July 23, 2018.

Alice Bowsman displays an honor she received from the State of Indiana commemorating Edwards Jewelers' one hundred years in business. *From the* Courier-Times.

With her youthful look and personality to match, some may find it hard to believe that Bowsman was a part of Edwards Jewelers through nearly half of its one-hundred-year existence. "I've been here forty-two years," Alice said in 2021 with a tone of disbelief in her voice.

The 1976 New Castle Chrysler High School graduate started working here when she was a senior. In fact, her high school schedule included not only teachers during the day but also a who's who of local merchants.

A daughter of Howard and Pat Millis, Alice worked for Morris Edwards at the jewelry store, for Beall's Dale Biddinger, jewelry store owner Warren Worl and shoe store fixture Bud Bunton. "They all shared me doing different jobs," Alice said. "I think they would flip a coin to see who would get me in their store that particular weekend."

Even after Bowsman left for college at Purdue University in pursuit of an art degree, she returned, working during breaks and summers in downtown New Castle. And when her art degree plans faded in favor of becoming a registered nurse, Bowsman was still drawn to the jewelry store like a magnet.

Above: This January 1951 photo shows Ray Edwards inside his office at the Edwards Jewelers store. More than seven decades later, the store was still operating at the same location, 1334 Broad Street, New Castle, until it closed in 2023 after 102 years in business. *Doug Magers*.

Left: Edwards Jewelers founder H. Ray Edwards stands next to his son, Morris. *Doug Magers*.

Mr. and Mrs. Warren Worl were downtown New Castle merchants for many years. Alice Bowsman credited them with being a positive business influence. *Digital collection of the late Mike Bertram.*

"I've just always loved downtown," Bowsman said. "It's personal to me. I think if you run something good, people will come to you no matter where you're located. I never even once thought about moving to the highway. I love the quaintness of downtown, and I love to be able to wait on my customers one on one. When I shop, I like places where I get waited on. You know, people can buy from the internet all they want, but there's nothing like customer service."

Today, Alice's education pursuits have come full circle with the business she loves. Her art education is evident in the custom-designed jewelry she offers. Lessons learned from downtown mainstays of the past have led a nurse-like care of a local institution to its milestone one-hundred-year achievement.

Her nursing education also influenced daughter Brittny Berry to become a registered nurse. Not only that, it also helped Alice's husband recover from a serious accident a few years ago. "My husband, Donnie, is my rock," Alice said of the man who once played a key role in leading New Castle to the basketball semi-state in the mid-'80s and is now superintendent of the Randolph Southern School Corporation. "While he doesn't participate in the everyday events of the store, he is always by my side, supporting and encouraging me to keep doing what I love to do."

Alice reached a wonderland status not thanks to a Mad Hatter, Cheshire Cat or White Rabbit; rather, it's been the Edwards Jewelers ability to adapt with change—both inside and outside the store. Nothing put that adaptability to the test more than the ongoing pandemic.

"We made ourselves adapt to the situation," Alice said. "We cut our hours back to save on expenses. I feel like we're doing OK. We'll get through this too."

But it certainly wasn't the first time Edwards Jewelers had faced rough times. "I can remember three times in my life where Broad Street was completely closed down," Alice said. "We had to think outside the box then, too."

The fighting spirit is in the DNA of the Edwards name. H. Ray Edwards, a World War I veteran, came to New Castle in 1920 following service overseas. He teamed with Coffin's Jewelry Store in the beginning but later opened his own store in the old Kahn-Heller building at the southeast corner of the Broad and Fourteenth intersection. Then Edwards bought Walter Burhman's business across the street at 1321 Broad Street and, for a time, operated the two stores.

"Both stores later were consolidated at the latter address and recently the store was moved to its present site, 1334 Broad, after extensive interior remodeling and installation of a modern glass front," late historian Herbert Heller wrote in his *Historic Henry County* three-volume set. "The Edwards establishment carries leading lines of watches, a large stock of diamonds, clocks and gifts and for some time has been one of the city's leading dealers in cameras and photographic supplies. Edwards himself is an enthusiastic and skillful amateur cameraman."

When the instant Polaroid cameras and film developing services became relics due to advancement of cellphone photography, the store had to change, challenging Alice's ability to come up with picture-perfect alternatives.

She remembers the skepticism of her old boss when delving into the fashion jewelry market. "When I first told Morris we were going to get fashion jewelry in, he wasn't sure about it," Alice remembered. "Then he saw how women wanted that. It drew different type of customers. So when I took over the store in the early 1990s, I did away with all the camera stuff."

James Edwards (*far right*) shows Steve Ditton, Dottie Eschenbrenner and Cindy James the latest in photography at Edwards Jewelers in this 1977 photo. *Digital collection of the late Mike Bertram.*

Meanwhile, as time marches on, ways to track it have changed dramatically—so much, in fact, that sale of watches, once a store staple, took a back seat to other items in the store. But as the saying goes, diamonds are forever.

"We still sell a big variety," Alice said before the store closed. "This has been a big year for custom designs. I do a lot of custom designs. People are bringing in their rings, and I'm designing new ones out of what they have. That's fun for me. I like doing that. That's my creativity."

Meanwhile, an array of different products can be found throughout the store, things that H. Ray Edwards would have never dreamed of stocking when he opened the store a century ago.

Edwards's popular Facebook page features everything from custom-designed wedding ring sets to recycled Crossbody Boho handbags, baseball-themed T-shirts and earrings, Brumate drinkware and more. Alice thinks that Morris and his dear wife, Shirley, would be pleased. She's grateful that the family name, which includes the Edwards's daughters Cathy and

Susan, continued to have a presence in a place that meant so much to them all for so long.

Among the smiling faces inside the store were living links to the past. Pat Williams worked for McCormack-Hammer, which for years operated on 14th Street. Linda Imel worked for Harmon Hoy Jewelers years ago. Alice's mom, Pat Millis, who worked at Purdue Extension and the high school years ago, is also background presence when needed.

Like a beautiful chain necklace, Alice cherishes the links former employees have with her efforts at the store over the years. "All of my co-workers over the years have meant so much," she said. "I love the fact that everyone who has ever worked at the store remains friends to this day. They are immeasurable treasures to me."

Alice refused to rest on laurels. To many downtown motorists, the vintage Edwards sign, restored to its full colorful self in 2014, was a local landmark. Thanks to the creative work of local merchants Jeff Smiley and Margison Graphics, the sign was updated and became "like a night beacon," Alice said.

Jewelry has a special kind of magic behind it that spans generations. Alice remembers the very first piece of jewelry she ever bought. "It was from Warren Worl," she said. "It was a chunky coral necklace. I have it on in my senior pictures. My mom and dad helped me get that. I still have it."

Many years from now, Alice hopes that others can reflect on the sparkle they found in their lives at this downtown beacon, a true survivor called Edwards Jewelers.

Krell-French Pianos: A Symphony of History and Spirit

"Oh look. There's a Krell-French piano." The words were said not by a music teacher or an antique dealer. They were said on the big screen, spoken by legendary actor Paul Newman in a film with Joanne Woodward.

In the early 1900s, everyone had heard of a Krell-French piano. A 1910 publication of the *Industrial Edition* said that the piano company had become one of the largest distributors of pianos and organs, "covering an area twice as large the German empire."

The story of the piano factory in New Castle plays like a Beethoven number, a stirring rendition of community spirit and successful risk-taking, one that served as a prelude to an industrial prowess that helped make New Castle the place to be at the turn of the twentieth century.

Interestingly, like the Hoosier Kitchen Cabinet factory that would come later, it all started with a fire. When a fire destroyed the Krell-French Piano Factory in Springfield, Tennessee, New Castle city leaders—led by Charles Hernly, a true economic developer long before the term ever came into existence—decided to lure the company here.

But it took $60,000 in cash and another $125,000 for preferred stock, as well as an equally large leap in faith. "The directors were neither stampeded nor frightened at the size of the deal," an article in the 1903 *New Castle Democrat* reported. "Calling in a few good citizens, they arranged to meet the piano company directors at Indianapolis on a certain day. Before that meeting was over, these eight or 10 men had signed a contract making themselves individually responsible for payment of the money."

It might have been perceived as a gamble at the time. But the end result produced a veritable symphony of noteworthy benefits for the town.

The Krell-French Piano Company would become one of the four largest in the United States. The plant itself contained more than five acres of floor space and employed more than four hundred skilled workers. Thousands of pianos were kept moving through the factory at all times in various stages of construction. An average weekly payroll of $4,500 was realized here, translating to an annual payroll of $250,000.

To say that the piano factory success was one of the keys to New Castle's early growth is an understatement. The population increased by as many as three thousand people—more than had come to town in the previous half century.

The ripple effects of the piano factory led to other monumental events in New Castle's history. Jesse French Sr., who bought out his partner and made it the Jesse French Piano Factory, contributed $45,000 to construction of a new YMCA on Church Street, a facility that opened in 1925 and served New Castle for more than seventy years. The building is no longer a Y but, as of 2023, was still in use as a community center.

In 1989, the Henry County Historical Society museum received a unique visitor. Elizabeth French Kelly, the daughter of Jesse French Jr. and granddaughter of company cofounder Jesse French Sr., visited the facility and spent some time around the vintage Jesse French piano featured in the museum's main room. Her son, Dr. Steve Kelly, had arranged the trip.

Dr. Kelly said then that even though the pianos aren't made anymore, they live on like a classic song. He told the story of a patient who, in casual

Henry County Historical Society has a vintage Jesse French piano that is still played for special occasions. *Henry County Historical Society*.

conversation, talked about buying an old piano on eBay. When asked where the piano originated, the patient said, "You wouldn't know, some little town in Indiana." Even more interested now, Kelly persisted, asking what brand it was.

"A Jesse French piano," was the reply.

"Why, that's my grandfather," Kelly said.

You can see an original Jesse French piano and learn more about its history at the Henry County Historical Society Museum, 606 South 14th Street. It's open from 1:00 p.m. to 4:30 p.m. Tuesday through Friday or by appointment, 765-529-4028.

HOOSIER KITCHEN CABINETS: FACTORY BROUGHT PROSPERITY, NATIONAL NOTICE AND EVEN HELPED NAME A STREET

"Kitchen pianos." "Cupboards with brains." "Scientific pantries." These are just a few of the phrases used to describe what was a modern marvel for housewives across America in the early 1900s: the Hoosier Kitchen Cabinet.

For forty years, some 4 million free-standing Hoosier Kitchen cabinets were made in New Castle. By 1921, one in ten U.S. homes had a Hoosier Kitchen Cabinet. Today, they are collector's items, and the Hoosier Kitchen Cabinet has a permanent place in the Henry County history book.

Originally, James S. and Emmett McQuinn were in business to sell "seed separators" to farmers via horse and wagon. They only started making kitchen cabinets as a way to occupy workers during the winter months. But soon, they discovered that the kitchen cabinets were far more popular than the seed separators.

New Castle's good fortune started with a tragic fire. In 1900, fire destroyed James S. McQuinn's Albany, Indiana factory. "Well, I guess it's all over now," son Emmett McQuinn said.

"No, it isn't all over," J.S. McQuinn replied. "We are just now getting a good start. This simply means that we will go to New Castle or some other place and go at it right."

The McQuinns headed to New Castle, where a $2,000 incentive was waiting for them. "We were then driven way out to Lewisville Pike to see the Speeder Cycle Company's factory, where bicycles were made from 1885 to 1900. As some of the citizens said at the time, 'It was located clear out beyond the old fairgrounds' and it did look like it was an awfully long ways from town. At that time, there were no sidewalks south of Circle Street and all land east of the road was farm land.…We were sure we wanted to locate in New Castle but the matter was still undecided. He and I finally concluded we would take one long chance that the deal would go through all right and that New Castle would be our new home."

The McQuinns were anxious to run a national advertisement, but when asked what address to put in the ad, they weren't sure. The old bicycle plant they were taking over was located on what was then known as Lewisville Pike. But the McQuinns didn't know that at the time.

"Well, we sent the ad in and gave the address of the company as 1200 South 14th St., New Castle, Ind. At that time, there was no 14th Street in New Castle, but 14th sounded as good to us as anything, so we used it. Some

Opposite: James McQuinn moved his factory from Albany, Indiana, to New Castle and shifted from production of seed separators to kitchen cabinets. *Henry County Historical Society*.

Above: This former bicycle factory was transformed into a place where millions of Hoosier Kitchen Cabinets were made. Today, they are collectors' items. *Digital collection of the late Mike Bertram*.

five or six years after we came here, the town board re-named the streets and Lewisville Pike became 14th Street," said J.S. McQuinn.

The Hoosier Kitchen Cabinet legacy includes far more than just naming a street, however. The Hoosier Kitchen Cabinet Company was said to be the first in the nation to offer a time-payment plan. For just one dollar per week, a homemaker could have one. The total retail cost was $49.50 in 1918, so in a year's time, a customer would have it paid off.

Peak employment included seven hundred men and women working at the factory, forty to fifty traveling salesmen and an office staff of sixty to seventy. During peak years, nearly seven hundred cabinets per day were produced. At one time, Hoosier was the largest manufacturer of kitchen cabinets in the United States.

As the years went by, Hoosier Kitchen Cabinets kept getting better and better. Features included flour bins with sifters, lined silver drawers, rustproof and—more importantly—mouse-proof cake drawers, mesh vegetable bins, pan racks, cookbook holders and sugar bins. Later models also included a

Here's an example of a Hoosier Kitchen Cabinet, designed to make cooking easier with its cleverly placed bins and accessories. *Henry County Historical Society.*

Above: At one time, the Hoosier Manufacturing Company facility in New Castle was the largest maker of kitchen cabinets in the United States. *Henry County Historical Society.*

Left: Many memorable ads were placed in the *Saturday Evening Post*, helping the Hoosier Manufacturing Company grow. *Henry County Historical Society.*

pencil holder by the flour bin, a clock-faced shopping list, a file for grocery bills and a money tray.

Like many things, changing times ultimately ended the Hoosier Kitchen Cabinet's reign of popularity. The late Betty O'Neal Giboney, a staff writer at the *Courier-Times* for forty-five years, wrote, "During the 1930s, wall cabinets had been introduced. Developers of apartment buildings which could place huge orders began using stationary wall cabinets, just as private homes were doing. Workers were changing, too, and they were becoming restless over wages. A strike was called. The elder McQuinn had died and his son was in charge. With no stomach for a labor dispute, E.Q. McQuinn sold the business in 1942 and it was subsequently liquidated by the purchasers. During World War II, the buildings were used as government warehouses."

But while the production ceased, the Hoosier Kitchen Cabinet lives on as true collector's items. An advertisement in the *Saturday Evening Post* said it all. "I too have abolished slavery," the headline read. The copy read, "Drudgery has ceased to be their master. With its many features and labor-saving inventions, the Hoosier has made their kitchen work easy and enjoyable."

Hoosier Kitchen Cabinets are on display at the Henry County Historical Society museum. The museum is open Tuesday through Friday from 1:00 p.m. to 4:30 p.m. each day and anytime by appointment. For more information, call 765-529-4028 or visit www.henrycountyhs.org.

Nip and Tuck: How a Chicken Dinner Blessed New Castle for Nearly a Century

When the phrase "nip and tuck" is used, often it's to describe an extremely close basketball game. But in New Castle's case, it was the catalyst for one of the greatest economic development triumphs of all time.

It was at the Nip and Tuck Club on the north edge of New Castle where early automobile makers Jonathan Maxwell and Benjamin Briscoe were wined and dined over a chicken dinner and convinced that New Castle, not Muncie, would be the best place for their factory.

That event in 1906 set the stage for tremendous growth in the city, the ripple of effects of which can even be felt today, more than one hundred years later.

The club, hosted by Colonel James Nipp, had a reputation for influencing the rich, famous and powerful. A newspaper article of that era revealed the prestige that James Nipp's club had achieved since opening it in 1899.

These members of the Nip and Tuck Club convinced Jonathan Maxwell and Benjamin Briscoe to pick New Castle over Muncie for their new factory. *Doug Magers.*

Here are excerpts from a September 21, 1903 article published by the *Indianapolis Star*:

> *When the history of Indiana Republicanism is again written, it cannot evade the name of Col. James Nipp. Colonel Nipp's title came not from service at the cannon's mouth, but from heroism at the sacred springs on his farm in Henry County. There, under the shade of sheltering sycamores, where the air is laden with the scent of abundant mint crop, and the wild rose rods, and the honey bee is surfeited, he had dedicated a monument to Indiana Republicanism.*
>
> *Colonel Nipp is the permanent "host" of the Nip and Tuck Club. Several years ago a number of well-known politicians of Henry County, inspired by former State Chairman Charles Hernly, Judge M.I. Forkner, Judge Eugene Bundy and others, habitually met at the Nipp spring and feasted on chicken. That was the only point in the program where Colonel Nipp gave way to Mrs. Colonel Nipp. The colonel's particular responsibility rested on mint julep.*
>
> *Three years ago the Nip and Tuck Club organized with 25 members— one president and 24 vice presidents. Annual entertainments were begun, to which the politicians of Indiana—that is the Republicans—were invited.*

Some regard it as political suicide for the ambitious to ignore the summons and Governors, Senators and Congressmen obey.

The "Nip" in the country club name was a clever play on words emphasizing the commonly used sports term but actually represented a well-known local name, Nipp, as in the family of former New Castle mayor Tom Nipp. Nipp, his brother Jim and son John discussed the historical significance of their ancestor's club with the *Courier-Times*.

"They said doctors and lawyers would get on the train, ride here, go to the club and party some days, then get back on the train, go home in the evening and their families never knew," Tom Nipp said.

"It was mentioned on the Congressional Record," John Nipp added. "They would come from all over the country because they had Nipp Springs, a mill and a train depot that was not too far from the country club."

Charles Hernly was no stranger to the club—literally and figuratively. It was Hernly who, in a manner of speaking, crashed a party in Muncie and invited the auto entrepreneurs to stop in New Castle before making their final decision.

"Muncie was primarily influenced by the Ball family and Ball Corp.," Tom Nipp explained. "The people who wanted to start the car manufacturing plant were looking at this area and the influence of the Balls snagged them, and I believe they had a signed agreement.

"But New Castle had an entrepreneur named Hernly who was influential in getting the Jesse French piano factory here and other things started to happen," Tom Nipp continued. "Somehow he got in touch with those people and persuaded them to just come down for a dinner.

Powerful national and state legislators were known to frequent the Nip and Tuck country club at the turn of the century. *Henry County Historical Society.*

In 2023, this was the remains of the Nip and Tuck Club. In 1906, a decision was made here that positively changed Henry County forever. *Doug Magers*.

What happened at the Nip and Tuck Club north of New Castle led to the largest automobile factory in the country at the turn of the twentieth century. *Henry County Historical Society.*

"They were famous for fried chicken at the country club, put on a great big spread and party for Maxwell and Briscoe, and persuaded them to tear up the agreement with Muncie and put the plant here."

Tom Nipp emphasized that it was local leaders like Hernly who were the keys; the Nip and Tuck Country was just the host. "The Nipps cooked the chicken," John added.

The setting was a scenic one. James Nipp, the founder, grew up in a family who built gristmills across Indiana. "They would scout streams that would be suitable for mills," John Nipp explained, saying that the family were responsible for more than sixty such mills in Indiana alone. "When people would go to the country club, they would turn off right where the power plant was for the state hospital, follow the river and go down across it," John Nipp explained. "It's back in the woods."

Maxwell and Briscoe were royally entertained and made the decision to make New Castle their new factory home. It became the largest manufacturing facility of its kind in the world when, as Richard Ratcliff wrote, "they planted an automobile factory next to 2,500 farms." The factory helped New Castle grow in both population and stature. It was the economic engine that moved New Castle and its people for nearly a century.

And it all started over a chicken dinner.

WHEN NEW CASTLE BECAME "ROSE CITY," NATIONAL FAME, LOCAL FORTUNES GREW LIKE THE FLOWER

They were everywhere. Five of them were just southwest of the General William Grose home on South 15th Street. Others could be found on Indiana Avenue, West Broad, Spring, Vine and 25th Streets. In fact, at one time, there were as many as one hundred of them here—greenhouses nurturing special kinds of roses, literally helping New Castle grow and bloom.

Verification of New Castle's "Rose City" roots were uncovered by a special 1910 magazine edition of the *New Castle Daily Times*. "New Castle, the Rose City. The name has spread over the country and the name Rose City has become almost as firmly attached to New Castle as has the Windy City to Chicago and the Golden Gate City to San Francisco," the 1910 edition said.

Names like Heller, Weiland and Meek became famous back then. The Rose City tradition lives on today in local flower shops bearing the Weiland name. The Rose Bowl on Indiana 3, a bowling alley and entertainment center, honors the flowering heritage of the town.

In today's current economic challenges, it may be hard for some to believe that the American Beauty Rose grown here actually became a symbol of wealth alongside mink coats and diamonds. They were sold for thirty-six dollars per dozen at Chicago, a hefty price back then. That was promptly doubled for retail. For special occasions, they were cut as tall as twelve feet high.

One town resident, Mrs. Carl Irwin, wrote that "lucky indeed was the girl who could stand at her graduation or wedding with American Beauty Roses in her arms." The New Castle roses were featured in such national magazines as the *Ladies Home Journal*.

"Thousands are sent out every day during the season but even then the demand is greater than the supply," a 1910 story in the *New Castle Democrat* reported. "It seems strange that in mid-winter New Castle roses should be sent to Memphis, Mobile and New Orleans and other southern cities where flowers grow the year round but such is a fact."

Historians point to brothers Myer and Herbert Heller for planting the seeds of New Castle's rose-colored triumphs. "Instead of growing a variety of flowers, they confined themselves to the culture of roses exclusively," a 1903 *New Castle Democrat* article stated. "American Beauties were their specialty and they took one prize after another at all the great flower shows in the country, until it became evident that the best roses in America were grown in New Castle."

Heller Bros. Company
New Castle, Indiana

Sec. 562, P. L. & R.

E. C. AUCHTER
U. S. DEPT OF AGRICULTO
WASHINGTON D.C.   RE

Roses of New Castle
for 1934

Sensational
Low Price!
TWO
2 yr. plants
for $1.25
Postpaid

The Superb New
"PRIDE OF
NEW CASTLE"
A new bush rose of
astounding beauty

NRA

Opposite: This advertisement from 1934 encouraged the purchase of the American Beauty Rose. At one time, the South Floral Company sold more than 1 million flowers per year. *Henry County Historical Society.*

Above, left: Myer Heller and his brother, Herbert, were the masterminds behind the American Beauty Rose. *Henry County Historical Society.*

Above, right: Herbert Heller and his brother, Myer, turned New Castle into the "Rose City." *Henry County Historical Society.*

With buds the size of goose eggs and an amazingly high petal count, the American Beauty was an instant hit. Long before there were celebrations in the streets over basketball triumphs, New Castle residents were whooping it up over roses. Mrs. Irwin recalled that when Myer Heller sent word that the New Castle roses had won the Kansas City contest, the town went wild.

"Strangers grabbed each other on the streets and local people who had once thought the greenhouse men an odd breed greeted them as brothers," she wrote. "Someone grabbed a fiddle and they put on a celebration the town was long to remember."

Giant red roses meant lots of green for New Castle. The Rose City heritage was a legitimate economic driver in a town already known for its industrial prowess with the Maxwell Automobile factory.

A cruel combination of natural and man-made forces ultimately spelled the demise of New Castle's flower power. The 1917 tornado leveled many

Workers sit amid the rubble following a March 11, 1917 tornado. While the city was once home to more than one hundred greenhouses, headlines proclaimed "Rose City in Ruins." *Digital collection of the late Mike Bertram.*

of the greenhouses here. News of the disaster was published as far away as St. Louis, where readers saw the headline "The Rose City Now a City of Ruins."

Local historians also pointed to World War I, which severely limited the export business. Competition from the Hill Floral Company in Richmond also made it hard for the American Beauty Rose to survive. That company produced roses that, while not nearly as spectacular, were much cheaper.

So the American Beauty Rose ultimately faded from view. But almost one hundred years later, it's important to remember that New Castle was Indiana's original "Rose City."

DISEASE

SMALLPOX LOOMED LARGE IN NEW CASTLE NEARLY ONE HUNDRED YEARS AGO

New Castle residents were anticipating one of the biggest celebrations in the town's young history. Then disease took over.

Those lamenting over changed plans and canceled events due to the 2020 COVID-19 pandemic are certainly not unique. Almost one hundred years ago, a grand celebration about the arrival of a piano factory here was canceled. The culprit was called smallpox, but its deadly impact was huge.

Thanks to the files of New Castle historian Doug Magers, we have a glimpse of those days filled with the pain and disappointment that followed.

From a February 4, 1903 New Castle newspaper article:

> *The County Commissioners met today and placed quarantine against Dublin (a town 14 miles southeast of New Castle) where several cases of smallpox has appeared. This was done at the insistence of the Dublin Township Trustee.*
>
> *At Dublin, three cases of smallpox were discovered Monday and so many persons have been exposed that the town is greatly alarmed.*
>
> *In Indianapolis, there have been 500 cases and 50 deaths this winter from the disease and all the school children have been ordered vaccinated.*

Like its automobile and kitchen cabinet factories, New Castle also boasted of having one of the largest piano manufacturing facilities in the nation. *Henry County Historical Society.*

Also, Henry County Commissioners passed a resolution for every person in Henry County to be vaccinated immediately. O.P. Hatfield and Dr. Harvey Koons were appointed to select four guards to be placed on the roads leading into Henry County from Dublin and no one is to pass or re-pass.

The formal opening of the piano factory, which was to have taken place next Tuesday, Feb. 10, will not be held. This action was taken at the request of the County Board of Health, who feared some of the thousands of people expected that day might come from towns infested with smallpox, with the result that it might be brought to New Castle.

The County Commissioners today passed a resolution for every person in Henry County to be vaccinated immediately. Those who are not able to pay may go to any doctor who will charge them nothing. The physician will file his bill with the county, which will pay 50 cents for each person.

The Centers for Disease Control reported that on average, three out of every ten people who got it died. Those who survived were usually left with scars, which were sometimes severe. Just seven days after the initial newspaper report, the loss of the Krell-French Piano event was lamented in the February 10, 1903 *Courier* but not questioned:

New Castle has missed the biggest event in all her history and that through no fault of any person or persons, the opening of the Krell-French Piano Factory would have been an event of a lifetime today. New Castle has missed a big thing and the general prevalence of smallpox over the county is to blame. The urgent requests from people in general that the event be postponed and however much everybody regretted the necessity for such action, it seemed the best thing to do under the circumstances.

The Krell-French Piano Company would become one of the four largest in the United States. The plant itself, located where many remember Modernfold, contained more than five acres of floor space and employed more than four hundred skilled workers.

The location of the Krell-French Piano Company was said to be a major event in the climax of the industrial movement here. A single institution employing five hundred people meant an increase in population of between two thousand to three thousand people. That was more new people for New Castle than had come to town in the past century.

The loss of a grand opening celebration turned out to be just a footnote for a piano company's stirring legacy.

Remembering the Holland Family Tragedy

So much can happen in a five-year period, especially where families are concerned. Change and growth happen right before a parent's eyes. Relationships deepen. The future becomes eagerly anticipated. But for the Joshua Holland family of New Castle, a five-year period between 1867 and 1872 proved tragic because of two terrible letters that struck fear across the world at that time: TB.

All five of the Holland children died in a five-year span from March 1867 through 1872. They ranged in age from twenty-two to twenty-six at the times of their death. Their only descendant, Tucie Murphy, a granddaughter of Joshua and Nancy Holland, died in 1875 at the age of eighteen. Miraculously, their parents survived through it all, living to bury each one of their dear children.

Joshua Holland was a well-known citizen at that time. He was a New Castle merchant who once served as county treasurer and co-superintendent of the Henry County seminary.

Holland Elementary School was built in the early 1900s. It was named in memory of a family who lost five children to tuberculosis. *Henry County Historical Society.*

Formerly called "consumption," tuberculosis (TB) is characterized externally by fatigue, night sweats and a general "wasting away" of the victim. By the dawn of the nineteenth century, tuberculosis had killed one in seven of all people who had ever lived.

Thankfully, tuberculosis is no longer the threat it once was. According to the Centers for Disease Controls, the number of tuberculosis cases and incidences in the United States have steadily declined since 1993.

The site of the Holland home on West Broad Street in downtown New Castle has undergone two significant transitions since those fateful years. At a meeting of the school board in 1907, officials agreed to explore purchase of the Joshua Holland house on West Broad Street. This was initiated the following year.

Holland became one of six new elementary schools constructed in New Castle between 1907 and 1910 to accommodate a population that had doubled in a decade. The list included Hernly (1907), Holland (1910), Parker (1911), Bundy (1912) and Riley (1917).

"Thus it was that Holland School, built on the site of the home, was dedicated to the education of youth in remembrance of the tragedy and grief of the Holland family," late New Castle historian Herbert Heller wrote in his *Historic Henry County* books. Sadly, the school lasted much longer than the family.

Today, the school is long gone, but "family" is still front and center at the site, where the Dollar General Store has been located for many years now. The store offers local families an economical way to shop, enabling them to get the most for their money. For those who know the Holland story, the site also reminds us daily of our modern medical blessings protecting that which is priceless.

LEWISVILLE MAN FACED 1918 PANDEMIC HEAD ON

Anyone who thinks that things are bad now with the COVID-19 pandemic needs a history lesson—perhaps even more than mass quantities of toilet paper.

The year was 1918. An influenza pandemic had arrived in the United States. Most believed that it originated in China. According to the Centers for Disease Control and Prevention, it is estimated that about 500 million people, or one-third of the world's population, became infected with this virus. More people died from the flu virus than were killed in combat during World War I.

Howard Caldwell Jr. was an iconic television broadcaster for Indianapolis TV station WRTV. His family roots extended to Henry County, Indiana. *WRTV, Indianapolis.*

The late Howard Caldwell Jr., who became one of the most trusted Indianapolis television journalists while working for WRTV for thirty-five years, had a unique link to stories connected with the 1918 pandemic. His father, Howard Caldwell Sr., was serving in the U.S. Navy during World War I. And Howard Caldwell Sr. happened to be from Lewisville, right here in Henry County.

The late TV broadcaster's daughter, Ginny Hingst, recently shared some letters with now retired State Representative Tom Saunders (another Lewisville son) written by her grandfather during the height of the 1918 pandemic. Those letters and a column written by the late broadcast icon in 2002 shined a light on a truly dark time, one to this point we haven't even come close to repeating.

In Howard Jr.'s 2002 print column "Howard Caldwell Remembers," the Channel 6 legend offered a vivid description of what things were like during that crisis, according to a November 19, 1918 issue of the *Indianapolis Star*.

"The citizens of Indianapolis learned they would be required to wear protective facemasks," Caldwell wrote. "Only exceptions were when they were at home, or when eating, or when they were 'on the street.'"

Caldwell said that people were required to wear protective face masks while in any store, office, factory, public building, theater, church, streetcar or any public gathering place. If you needed a haircut, both you and the barber would have to wear masks. If you went into a public office, both you and the clerk would have to wear masks. If you went into a restaurant, both you and the waiter would have to wear masks.

"Early in October, local officials became convinced that Indianapolis and surrounding counties should impose precautionary measures. On Oct. 7, a *Star* headline announced that effective immediately, all schools, churches, theaters and amusements of all kinds and other public gathering places would be closed to the public," Caldwell wrote. Sound familiar?

Gratitude and positive thinking seem to pour from Howard Caldwell Sr.'s handwritten letters to his mother, Martha, who lived in Lewisville, and his wife, Elsie, as fear gripped the entire world. The Lewisville man considered himself "one of the lucky ones"—in more ways than one.

"I know you are anxious to learn how I am withstanding Spanish influenza," Caldwell Sr. wrote. "I'm glad to report I am still on the lucky list."

Before it was over, the number of deaths from the Spanish flu was estimated to be at least 50 million worldwide, with about 675,000 occurring in the United States. Mortality was high in people younger than five years old, those between twenty and forty years old and those sixty-five years and older. The high mortality in healthy people, including those in the twenty to forty age group, was a unique feature of the 1918 pandemic.

Contrast that with the estimated 3 million who died worldwide during COVID-19 and you have a sad perspective on the scope of what happened in 1918.

Caldwell Sr. had already stared potential tragedy in the face, both in his personal and military life. His wife, Elsie, got the flu while she was pregnant and went into labor two months early. Both mother and daughter survived. But that was not the case for the naval officer Caldwell Sr. reported to at the Great Lakes Naval Training Center along Lake Michigan. The officer died from the flu, and Caldwell Sr. took his place.

The elder Howard Caldwell wrote reassuringly to his mother, Martha, soon afterward, not wanting her to worry. She had already lost her husband to pneumonia a few years earlier. "Mother, I'm feeling fine," Caldwell Sr. wrote. "Fact is, I never felt better in my life, and I'm leading a happy-go-lucky outdoor life. The war news is encouraging and I know you are heralding it with joy."

Caldwell Sr.'s bride, Elsie, whom he married just a few months earlier on March 24, 1918, received these words:

My darling Elsie,

You'd be interested to know, I'm sure, that the conveniences and privilege of my new job continues to tickle my sense of appreciation. One of the things that impresses me particularly is the mere opportunity that I am enjoying now of sitting down to my own desk in my own room and penning a letter in privacy to my little honey.

A surprise arrival had also lifted Caldwell Sr.'s spirits. "While marching a squad of rookies this afternoon, a voice hailed me out of a bunch of new arrivals," Caldwell, Sr. wrote. "I caught my first glimpse of Albert McIlvaine." Albert McIlvaine Jr. was also from Lewisville.

While he never became ill himself, Howard Caldwell Sr. faced the dangerous flu bug every day during the 1918 pandemic as he helped fellow shipmates afflicted with the disease.

LETTERS FROM SAILOR REVEAL DEPTH OF 1918 PANDEMIC

Howard Caldwell Sr. was serving on a U.S. naval base near Chicago, yet he found himself surrounded by a foreign enemy—a microscopic army of germs known as the Spanish flu. Those germs created a pandemic the likes of which the world had never seen.

As reports, debates and precautionary measures about the spread of COVID-19 made daily headlines, a series of dramatic, heartfelt and poignant letters from a local man in 1918 provide perspective and perhaps a bit of comfort concerning the pandemic of 2020.

Shared by granddaughter Ginny Hingst, the letters written by Caldwell reveal just how dire circumstances were with the Spanish flu, historic conditions that, so far, have not repeated themselves here with COVID-19:

Thursday, September 19, 1918

My dearest Elsie,

Just got my washing out—12 handkerchiefs, a suit of light underwear and one white hat, which brings me to the end of another perfect day in the Navy. We have discarded whites and now that blues are the uniform of the day, wash parties are a bit fewer. Twenty of our men are now in "sick bay." The illness is similar to grippe, except that the throat is sore. It is accompanied by a high fever and care must be taken to prevent pneumonia from developing. It is quite likely the camp will be under quarantine tomorrow.

Sunday, September 22, 1918

There was little or no liberty this weekend. None of the men in the detention camps went ashore and I understand liberty was restricted all over the station. A hard fight is being waged to get the influenza epidemic under control. I am busier than a cranberry merchant these days, as our company commander is sick and we have no second p.o. as yet.

Thursday evening, September 26, 1918

My dearest Elsie,

Yesterday was as happy a birthday as I could have had under the circumstances. It really was quite remarkable how near you and I seemed as I feasted on those two heavily ladened boxes of goodies. Both boxes arrived the day before. They not only made me very happy but they brought joy and ecstatic comments from several of my mates. I just finished mother's box this evening and have a few square pieces of your fruit cake left. I'm afraid I shan't be able to avail myself of your advice to "let it sweeten up" a week or so. I'm mighty glad you didn't have any wasted space around the edges of the cake, either. That candy helps wonderfully to bolster me up.

Caldwell would certainly need his strength in the days ahead. In another letter, Caldwell wrote there were seventy-seven deaths at the naval base over a twenty-four-hour period. Things were also bad at home. According to the website Indiana Disasters, the peak of the flu pandemic in the Hoosier State was October 1918. But what saved Indiana then might just help save Hoosiers now.

"Relative to elsewhere, the flu was not as severe," the website said. "This is due to specific measures that were taken, and even more direct measures that were taken by local governments. These measures not only likely saved lives, but it also helped remove the threat of the pandemic quicker than elsewhere." Those actions included restricting public meetings; limiting gatherings that included school, funerals and even church services; and sending workers home who were coughing or showed other symptoms.

Interestingly, many of those same actions were implemented by local leaders at the outbreak of the modern pandemic. Perhaps the history of the 1918 pandemic won't be repeated here because of them.

Somehow, Howard Caldwell Sr. didn't get sick in 1918. His survival made a significant difference, not only to the small town of Lewisville but also to the entire state. He would live to come home and raise a family, including a son named Howard Caldwell Jr., a man who was destined to become a television broadcasting legend in Indiana. But what he saw firsthand no doubt scarred him for the rest of his life.

1918 Pandemic Makes Its Way to New Castle

On Saturday, October 5, 1918, a small notice appeared near the bottom of the front page of the *Daily Courier*. Almost lost in the layout jumble of the day's news was a headline that read "Nurses Wanted at Once."

"Graduate, undergraduate nurses, nurses' aides register at once with the local Red Cross nursing committee for service in the present epidemic of influenza," the article read. "Volunteer service is greatly desired, but expenses and $75 a month will be paid to graduate nurses. Expenses and from $30 to $50 a month is the pay for undergraduates and nurses' aids."

It would be the first of many more articles, each growing in size and priority, as the 1918 Spanish flu pandemic began making its way to Henry County.

Just two days later, on Monday, October 7, 1918, a headline—far smaller than the large black World War I–related words at the top—read, "No Epidemic of Influenza Here." Local officials were so confident in this view that they convinced Indiana government officials to exempt Henry County from a state order closing public gatherings, schools and churches.

"The Spanish influenza epidemic sweeping the country is not serious enough in Newcastle to warrant the closing of all schools, churches and places of amusement and the dispensing of all public gatherings and the general order of state health authorities will not apply here for the present," the article read. "The order of the State Board of Health asking such action was contained in a telegram received this morning by city and county health officials, and for a time, it appeared certain that all schools, churches, and theaters would have to be closed. Mayor Elliott immediately got in communication with the State Board of Health and after explaining the situation here, was told that it would not be necessary to follow the order as long as people follow the necessary precautions."

George Elliott, New Castle's fourth mayor, had major decisions to make during the 1918 pandemic. *City of New Castle.*

New Castle's mayor at the time was George Elliott, who was a well-known local newspaper editor. The *Courier* acknowledged that "there are several cases here but the people have been observing the rules laid down and there is no occasion for any hysteria."

Mayor Elliott offered words of encouragement in the article:

All "safety first" measures possible are being used in Newcastle to avoid an epidemic of influenza and with the promise and proper cooperation of everybody, there should be none. For the past two weeks, all physicians have been required to report all cases of grippe or influenza to the secretary of the City Board of Health, who has promptly quarantined all such cases. In the schools, Supt. E.J. Llewelyn has barred from the rooms all teachers and pupils suffering with colds or headaches and the school buildings have been thoroughly fumigated three times each week.

I have asked all moving theater managers to bar from their places of amusement all persons suffering with coughs or colds and they will refuse to sell tickets to such. I ask all such persons not to attend public gatherings of any sort, and let us all strive and work together in an effort to avoid a spread of the epidemic to and in our city, and thereby avoid the necessity of closing our schools, churches and theaters. There have been and still are several cases of influenza in the city—probably from 40 to 50 in all—but they have been diagnosed as of the mild type and no deaths have occurred.

Unfortunately, however, there would be real-life drama ahead concerning the Spanish flu, despite the newspaper's reassuring words. "The people can aid greatly by taking proper care of themselves and by giving prompt attention to the mildest kind of cold, for right there is where the trouble always starts," the *Daily Courier* reported.

On Tuesday, October 8, the flu story headline, positioned a little higher on the front page this time, read, "SITUATION UNCHANGED. NO INDICATION OF INFLUENZA EPIDEMIC IN THE CITY."

"The influenza situation in New Castle remains unchanged over Monday and health officials declare the disease apparently does not gain any momentum here," the article said. "No new cases of influenza were reported to Dr. Fugate, secretary of the board of health today. The few cases that are here are confined to in a limited number of homes. For instance, 13 cases here are in three families and four cases are in two other families, showing the disease is not spreading. With the public obeying the suggestions of the health officials about staying indoors with colds and avoiding sneezing in public places, no epidemic is feared here."

But as time and the pandemic wore on, New Castle and Henry County would indeed need more nurses.

DOCTORS, NOT MASKS, WERE IN SHORT SUPPLY DURING 1918 PANDEMIC

When the flu pandemic of 1918 started to spread its wings and sweep across the country, the critical shortage wasn't masks or ventilators. It was availability of doctors.

During the third week of October 1918, front-page headlines of the *Daily Courier*—which had been encouraging and calm—started to take on a more dire tone. Flu headlines, which had been positioned in the middle or lower part of the front page, suddenly popped up at the top. "Flu Epidemic Only the Beginning," read a headline from October 18, 1918. "Reports of Surgeon General Rupert Blue Not Very Assuring" followed as subhead.

Still, at that time, the *Daily Courier* reported that New Castle had been fortunate with only six deaths. But the flu bug was spreading into the county, and a ban of public gatherings, similar to what was in place in modern times, was in full effect.

"So far, the city and the county have been fortunate as compared with other parts of the state," the newspaper reported. "This is the start of the third week on the ban and an extension depends largely on the public."

Meanwhile, the big news revolved around an October 21 front-page story highlighting a doctor shortage across Indiana. The pandemic came at a vulnerable time for the United States, which was also in the final stages of fighting in World War I. And that war demanded doctors too.

"In an effort to combat the epidemic, physicians have been asked to volunteer for work in other parts of the state," the *Courier* reported. "A meeting was held last Saturday at the clinic of all remaining physicians in the county and the question was discussed. In some communities in the state, so many physicians have been called into army service that the shortage is making it difficult to fight the epidemic."

"Under the plan, communities that had plenty of doctors have been asked to let some of them go to the harder-hit communities," the newspaper reported. Ultimately, four Henry County doctors volunteered their services elsewhere.

While the COVID-19 pandemic was cause for wall-to-wall national media coverage, the flu pandemic of 1918 took a back seat media-wise to World War I coverage. Big bold letters seemed to scream the news, "Allies Capture German Submarine Base," dwarfing news below it that a "Ban Likely to Be Continued" concerning the flu outbreak.

Of course, they were very different media times. With no televisions, no CNN or MSNBC or Fox News, the big story reporting was up to newspapers. But Howard Caldwell Sr. of Lewisville was not reading about the pandemic. He was living it.

Indiana TV Legend Shared Dad's Pandemic Experience

His parents had Lewisville roots. His award-winning journalism path actually began in Hagerstown at a weekly newspaper called *The Exponent*. Before his career was over, Howard Caldwell Jr. was regarded as an Indianapolis television icon and was later inducted into the Indiana Broadcast Hall of Fame.

But had his father, Howard Caldwell Sr., not miraculously withstood the Spanish flu pandemic of 1918, none of this would have happened. Ginny Hingst, the television broadcaster's daughter, would not have been born. And poignant letters about Howard Sr.'s experience would never have been shared.

So much would have changed. So much did change for others during that pandemic, which Caldwell Jr. wrote infected 25 percent of America's and proved fatal to 500,000 Americans. So much is changing and could continue to change for people today in the wake of the COVID-19 pandemic.

A column written by the broadcast legend in November 2002 and shared by Hingst through now retired State Representative Tom Saunders provided a vivid picture of what life was like back then—and perhaps another reason to follow "stay at home" orders during the COVID-19 pandemic.

While Marion County, Indiana, had 1,956 confirmed cases of COVID-19 early in 2020, Caldwell Jr. wrote that the number was 3,500 during the Spanish flu pandemic of 1918. The flu killed nearly 100 in Indianapolis alone. The Indiana Department of Health reported 4,944 positive COVID-19 cases statewide in April 2020, a number that approached the more than 6,000 flu cases that Caldwell Jr. reported as being treated statewide in 1918.

One particular warning in his 2002 column dealt with relaxing too early. According to Caldwell Jr., pressure from theater owners and other entertainment outlets may have influenced a removal of a ban in early October of that year when "all schools, churches, theaters and amusements of all kinds and public gathering places" were closed to the public. The ban was lifted at the end of October.

"It turned out to be premature," Caldwell Jr. wrote. "Days later, World War I ended. Parents, wives and children welcomed home the uniformed survivors. The influenza-pneumonia numbers soared thus precipitating the flu mask order in November of 1918. That order also called for continued closures of schools and libraries."

"In an attempt to ease the situation somewhat, the public was told that the masks could be purchased for no more than 10 cents apiece," Caldwell Jr. added. "Newspapers also provided instructions on how to assemble a mask, assuring that five or six could be assembled with necessary materials costing no more than 25 cents."

Caldwell Jr. reported that a mere five days after the mask move was initiated, it was announced that classes at all schools would resume the following Monday and that libraries would reopen that Friday. Again, it proved too soon. "A few days later, 167 new cases were reported in the city," Caldwell Jr. wrote. "Immediately unidentified critics blamed doctors for making late reports, creating misleading numbers."

Even after the 1918 pandemic began to calm down in Marion County, it spread to other areas of Indiana. Caldwell noted that the *Indianapolis Star* reported then "big outbreaks in 45 other Indiana counties with an average daily gain of 64 cases per county each day."

For the Caldwell family, the 1918 Spanish flu pandemic had a happy ending. "On Dec. 9, my sister was born in Indianapolis, two months premature," Caldwell Jr. wrote. "Mother had been diagnosed with the flu. Both mother and Virginia survived. A worried father, my dad—Howard Sr.—was serving in the U.S. Navy at the time. He was stationed at the Great Lakes Naval Training Center along Lake Michigan when the epidemic moved through the Midwest….He never became ill, and thus, along with many others, helped fellow shipmates who were seriously afflicted."

Happy endings for the current COVID-19 pandemic may well depend on how serious the general public views the situation.

FROM PANDEMIC FEAR TO HAPPY PANDEMONIUM

Headlines in the *Daily Courier* on Friday, November 8, 1918, reflected how New Castle had at last gone from pandemic to happy pandemonium, from deadly disease to celebration, from war to peace. Miraculously, World War I and the 1918 Spanish flu pandemic seemed to fade in favor of Americans at the same time.

"New Castle Held Real Celebration," headlines in the newspaper shouted. "City Certainly Demonstrated the Way Yanks Would March through Berlin," a subhead read. "Pandemonium Reigned," a third subhead proclaimed. "Traffic Blocked and Parade Moved with Difficulty," a fourth subhead stated.

"Premature or not, Newcastle and Henry County celebrated the end of the World War," the story noted. "Thursday night, bedlam broke loose for sure as the crowds which literally swarmed in the downtown district gave a demonstration never before equaled here. Thousands were on the street, shouting, firing revolvers, shot guns and making a noise with most ever imaginable device. The bands played 'A Hot Time in the Old Town' and 'Hail, Hail, the Gang's All Here.'"

Howard Caldwell Sr. and his Lewisville friend Albert McIlvaine weren't "here" just yet. But they were both survivors in a battle of a different kind, having somehow dodged the deadly flu that had ravaged their Great Lakes Naval Training Center.

This 1918 street scene shows the celebration after World War I ended. One of the national military heroes was New Castle's own General Omar Bundy. *Henry County Historical Society.*

In letters to his mother just a few weeks earlier, Caldwell Sr. was ever-encouraging about the health of himself and McIlvaine. "You wouldn't know your son to see him out on the drill field with about 70 blue jackets marching in his wake, executing squads right on the right into line, etc. I shall endeavor to get a picture of the company soon for your approval. We received colors today for our regiment. We passed in review at the Main Camp and impartial comments went to the effect that our company pulled down high honors. Constant drilling every morning and afternoon with the exception of Saturday and Sunday soon whips the most impossible rook into a remarkably rhythmic marching machine."

While Albert wasn't part of his unit, Caldwell kept in touch with his friend. "It was quite amusing to hear Albert relate how 'by gosh' they were making a sailor out of him over in Camp Dewey, where he is now attending hospital apprentice school," Caldwell wrote. "He said his company underwent repeated terrific 'ballings' from the Goldbraid [officers] and they had to lay out bags for inspection every night this week until they learned how to roll clothes neat and keep every piece clean."

"He said a 'Goldbraider' grabbed him by the collar and wanted to know why he didn't have clean stripes. He was also instructed to snap out of them rookie leggings and look like something," Caldwell continued. "Yesterday, he was wearing white leggings."

Then, referring to his wife, the former Elsie Rebecca Felt of Greenfield, Caldwell wrote, "Elsie sent me a set of prints from the films I sent her several days ago to be developed. They proved even better than my anticipation. I am sending her an order for additional prints and she will have set made up for you. Tell Mrs. McIlvaine the one of Albert and me is a winner."

Meanwhile, the picture at home was coming into a healthier focus. The *Daily Courier*'s Saturday, November 2 headlines offered good news on both foreign and home fronts. Below a war-related headline shouting "Americans Drive Deep Wedge in German Lines," the much smaller words below it read, "Schools of City to Open Monday."

A day after the big celebration, headlines in the *Daily Courier* reported, "Flu Conditions Improve: Physicians Believe Epidemic Has Definitely Been Checked."

A flu ban was lifted, allowing city schools to open for the first time in three weeks and two days. "The reopening of churches Sunday was marked by large attendance and other public gatherings indicated that people here are not hysterical or alarmed over the situation. Supt. [E.J.] Llewelyn stated that all the teachers were present for the opening of school…and that the attendance was surprisingly large."

Even the Royal Theatre was running advertisements again in the newspaper, advising that it had reopened. "The lid is off, but we will protect our patrons by disinfecting our theatre daily," the ad advised while promoting the movie titled *Raffles, the Amateur Cracksman*, a show filled with "thrills, comedy and romance."

But the pandemic of 1918 had levied a personal toll on many in New Castle, as well as throughout the state, nation and world. Locally, as many as 337 cases and 24 deaths were reported in Henry County. More than 14,000 Hoosiers died across Indiana. It's been reported that the pandemic lasted just fifteen months but was the deadliest disease outbreak in human history, killing between 50 million and 100 million people worldwide.

Dr. Ward Canaday, one of the physicians here who left home to help others, no doubt carried what he saw with him the rest of his life. Canaday had worked in Boston and Rhode Island. He cautioned local officials against relaxing the public activity ban too early. To him, Indianapolis lifting its ban was no good reason to do the same here.

"Regarding the severity of the plague, Dr. Canaday said it was enough to bring gray hairs to a man's head to go through the scenes he had experienced and witnessed," the *Daily Courier* reported.

Nothing approaching the deadliness of this plague has ever before visited this country, he declared, the fatalities reaching as high as thirty percent or more. He says the situation was simply appalling. In Boston, all the usual means of burial were found inadequate and bodies were taken to cemeteries on drays, trucks, wagons and automobiles. Meanwhile in New York City on Tuesday of this week, the health authorities told Dr. Canaday as he passed through on his way home that fifteen hundred bodies then awaited burial and the graves were being made with steam shovels.

The malady was so extremely fatal that in many cases which came under Dr. Canaday's observation, there was only a period of a few hours between the appearance of the first symptoms and death and thousands died before a physician could reach them.

In an effort to stave off any recurrence of flu here, everyone entering theaters, stores, churches, factories, jitneys (a term for buses back then) and public places were required to wear face masks for a period of time.

Howard Caldwell Jr., the Hall of Fame television newsman for many years on WRTV Channel 6, wouldn't have been born had his father not survived the 1918 flu pandemic that surrounded him on that naval base.

Multiply Caldwell's story against the 675,000 Americans who lost their lives and you have a changed world of dreams unfulfilled, possible human contributions to society unrealized and would-be heroes and heroines unborn. A world that today should be filled with people counting their blessings if COVID-19 hasn't yet knocked on the doors of their lives.

Our thanks to former State Representative Tom Saunders, who connected the *Courier-Times* with Ginny Hingst, daughter of Howard Caldwell Jr. and granddaughter of Howard Caldwell Sr. We appreciate her sharing these personal letters with us.

MEMORABLE FACES AND PLACES

THE CARPENTERS COME TO NEW CASTLE

They were the biggest-selling group of the '70s. No fewer than ten of their singles went on to become million-sellers, and by 2005, the combined worldwide sales of their albums and singles well exceeded 100 million units.

On November 7, 1974, this duo who had taken the *Billboard* charts by storm were in New Castle. The Carpenters performed at the Fieldhouse that night. A recent *Courier-Times* Facebook survey proved that memories as big as the moment linger with many.

Karla Edson kept her ticket stub. The cost to see this world-renowned group was $5.50, with part of the money going to help buy new Trojan Marching Band uniforms.

"It was my very first concert," she said. "I remember it well. They came as a New Castle high school fundraiser for new band uniforms the marching band needed. Premier-Southern Tickets (I believe out of Cincinnati) was the promoter."

For the brother-sister team who blazed a musical trail with such hits as "Close to You" and "We've Only Just Begun," performing in the world's largest and finest fieldhouse presented a challenge. A document Edson shared noted that Richard Carpenter compared the Fieldhouse design to a teacup, with bleachers on the inside walls and the group at the bottom of the cup.

CARPENTER

Richard Carpenter, 27, will direct the instrumental backup group Thursday during the appearance of The Carpenters in New Castle Fieldhouse at 8 p.m. Richard began writing songs early in his career, and the success of the Carpenters, with his sister, Karen, as vocalist, has won them numerous awards and gold records. Three of his best known hits are "Goodby to Love," "Yesterday Once More," and "Top of the World." Tickets still are available at Chrysler High School for the performance and tickets will be sold at the door.

This brief article featuring Richard Carpenter appeared in the *Courier-Times* on November 7, 1974, advertising the Carpenters concert that evening in New Castle Fieldhouse. *From the Courier-Times.*

The challenge was especially daunting for stagehands. "There is no way to back a truck up to the stage and unload the equipment," Edson's document read. "Instead it must be brought from the top, down an aisle to the bottom."

It reportedly took forty stagehands to get the huge truckload of Carpenter equipment down the aisle to the stage. The biggest problem was the huge soundboard and the nine-foot concert grand. Edson said that it was, of course, an even bigger problem getting all of the equipment back up to the top.

But those who were there, like Marilyn (Jones) Horan, Loveda (Scrogham) Jones and Greg Gard, will never forget it. "It was my first real concert," said Horan, a 1975 graduate of Blue River Valley High School. "I loved Karen. She was so amazing. The funny thing is that my husband, Mike, whom I didn't know at the time, had seen them perform at Ball State the evening before. Because he was in the music program, he was able to be backstage. I am still jealous over that!"

"My beloved grandma took me to this concert!" said Loveda Scrogham Jones, another BRV alum. "It was my first real concert. I loved the Carpenters and wanted to be able to sing like Karen!"

"I was there in awe," Mooreland's Greg Gard said. "Then bought their album *The Singles* as my very first record purchase. I was 13 and listened to it every day for months. Who didn't have a crush on Karen Carpenter??"

Linda Madison, who for many years owned and operated Weiland's Flowers in New Castle, not only remembers the concert well, but she also helped decorate Richard and Karen's hotel room. "I remember doing a flower arrangement for them using one of their 45s for their stay at the Holiday Inn as it was known then," Madison said. "A group of friends from one of my wholesalers had me get tickets for them. It was very well attended, a big deal for them to come to New Castle."

Retired New Castle teacher Jeri Anice Gooding recalled how she and Phyllis Klipsch also helped. "As home ec teachers, we provided the snacks, our office couch and coordinated the things they asked for back stage," Gooding said. "I remember distinctly that they wanted grapes. So we found the biggest and best available. The concert was awesome!"

Meanwhile, Julie Brammer remembered how she and other New Castle music students actually performed with the Carpenters at one point during the show. "It was awesome as a young student getting to be up on that stage and singing with them," she said. "Never forget it!!"

Retired *Courier-Times* photographer John Guglielmi didn't see the duo here but said that he photographed them for a Binghamton, New York newspaper. He remembered how pleasant they were, particularly Richard Carpenter. "Karen's brother was very hospitable to us," Guglielmi said. "Karen answered a few questions but mostly hung with the band. Excellent show."

Others who posted on Facebook that they were at the New Castle Fieldhouse show included Randy Sorrell, Brenda (Margison) Bockover, Linda Ratcliff, Dennis York, Wendy Wilson, Debbie (Dorn) Durst, Dorothy Shopp and Vicky McWhorter Pryor, then a senior at New Castle who sat in the front row.

Also there was this writer, who was a senior at Blue River Valley High School at the time, alongside his sisters, Cheryl and Donna, who proved to be the coolest of big sisters by taking her younger siblings to the concert.

According to Ray Coleman's book *The Carpenters: The Untold Story*, the New Castle event was one of a staggering 203 concerts that the Carpenters performed in 1974. The year the Carpenters came to New Castle would be the peak of their productivity as far as live performances were concerned. The very next year, their show numbers dropped nearly in half, to only 118 concert dates, with another 46 shows getting canceled.

Health problems started to shadow both Karen and Richard. She died on February 3, 1983, less than a decade after performing here. Richard, regarded as the creative force behind the group's success, battled with an addiction to Quaaludes but recovered and has gone on to produce other successful recordings.

It's been nearly fifty years, but chances are, anyone who was at the world's largest and finest high school gymnasium that night would say they've never seen anyone perform finer music than Richard and Karen Carpenter. They melted our hearts and, for a few brief moments, made us feel like one of their hit songs—on "Top of the World."

New Castle Youths Sing with the Carpenters

"Hello, is this Julie?" The Holland Elementary School fifth-grader didn't recognize who was on the other end of the phone. "Well, this is Richard Carpenter, and I'm the brother of Karen Carpenter," the man said. "You've probably heard we're coming to New Castle Fieldhouse."

"Yes, I auditioned to be in the background group," the surprised youngster said, still not sure if a music superstar was actually talking to her or if someone was playing a joke.

"Well, I'd like for you to accompany us in a song," the man continued.

That was how one of the most exciting and extraordinary experiences of Julie Bennett Brammer's young life began. She did indeed join the Carpenters, one of the biggest-selling recording artists of the 1970s. She was on stage with eleven or so other local elementary students when they performed at New Castle Fieldhouse on November 7, 1974.

Today, nearly fifty years later, Brammer still marvels at the opportunity she had. "It was just such a highlight of my elementary years," she said. "Even looking back, it's almost surreal that I got to do that. I know it was quite an honor."

Brammer and her New Castle elementary choir mates sang background vocals for the Carpenters' rendition of "Sing." Now a veteran teacher at Westwood Elementary School, Brammer said that the words of this song, first performed on the PBS kids' show *Sesame Street*, still resonate:

> *Sing.*
> *Sing a song.*
> *Sing out loud, sing out strong.*
> *Sing of good things, not bad.*
> *Sing of happy, not sad.*
> *Sing.*
> *Sing a song.*
> *Make it simple to last your whole life long.*
> *Don't worry that it's not good enough for anyone else to hear.*
> *Just sing.*

A daughter of Harold and Helen Bennett, Julie didn't need a lot of encouragement to sing, particularly where the Carpenters were concerned. "My mom was just so tickled for me," Brammer said. "She knew how much I liked the Carpenters."

New Castle resident Julie Brammer had the opportunity to sing with the Carpenters during a song performed at a November 7, 1974 concert. *Julie Brammer.*

Growing up in a family who had lots of love but little money, Brammer remembers how both her mother and her elder brother, Joe, made sure she was ready for the big performance. "I remember distinctly how mom took me up to Horney's Music Store on Race Street and told me to go in and get the 45rpm record of 'Sing' because I needed to practice," Brammer said.

"My brother, Joe, bought me a phonograph prior to the concert," she continued. "So that's where I would be every day after school, in my bedroom listening to the 45s of the Carpenters I got at Horneys."

Brammer also recalled that in spite of her family's tight budget, her mom made sure that a new outfit was purchased just for the concert. "I had six brothers and we were pretty poor," Brammer remembered. "So to go get a new outfit that wasn't Christmas or your birthday, that was a big deal."

"So we went to Arlan's Department Store [where Buffalo Wild Wings and Family Dollar are now]," Brammer continued. "She bought me a pair of canary yellow velour bell-bottoms. They were popular back then."

And another treat fit for a concert moment: a trip to the Sagittarius Plum. It was a popular clothing store across from the golf course along Indiana 3. "She found me a cute shirt there," Brammer said. "I was so excited because it was a very expensive store and you didn't go there unless you were rich. I felt like I was on top of the world."

Before the show began, Julie and her parents got to go backstage and actually meet Richard and Karen Carpenter. "That was the highlight of my life then," Julie said. "That was a big, big deal. I was nervous and excited. I just thought Karen Carpenter was the most amazing performer and still think her voice is like none other."

The aura of that Carpenters experience on that special night has followed Julie through the years. When she and husband Jeff were married thirty-five years ago, one of the songs performed by a friend was "We've Only Just Begun" from the Carpenters.

Even now, family get-togethers still don't end until Brammer performs. "It became a family tradition," she said. "I had six brothers, and I was the youngest, so I was surrounded by boys. At Christmas and different get-togethers, I would sing a song with a karaoke machine, and they would back me up. I was like Gladys Knight, and they were my Pips. Every time we get together, someone says 'OK, we've got to see Gladys Knight and the Pips."

Then there's how close friends continue to introduce her. "Maribeth Taylor, a good friend of mine, always says 'This is my friend Julie and she sang with the Carpenters,'" Brammer laughed.

As the years have gone by, mention of the Carpenters unfortunately draws puzzled faces from today's youth. But the relentless march of time has no power on the memory of a melody or a great experience. Nearly five decades later, the Carpenters continue to bring an occasional tear to her eye and instant goosebumps when she hears a familiar song on the radio, especially this time of year.

"When I hear Christmas songs by the Carpenters, I still get cold chills because it brings me back to that evening," Brammer said.

Seeing Some Famous Visitors Along the Trail

Called the "granddad of long-distance trails in Indiana," it's a shame that the sixty-two-mile-long Cardinal Greenway can't speak. Oh the stories this granddad could tell.

Tales ranging from the time Winston Churchill's son was in the northeastern Henry County area would no doubt be regaled. Then there's the more recent memory of how Indianapolis Colts quarterback Andrew Luck used the smooth surface to get back in shape following an injury. Or how the trail literally saved the life of a Henry County man, Darrell York, helping him lose one hundred pounds just by walking it regularly.

The old stone "W" sign seen along the trail would be explained. There'd also be talk of more recent sights—bald eagles, a family of foxes and the wide variety of bicycles now seen here that would make even the Wright brothers' eyebrows rise.

At the trailhead in the tiny town of Blountsville, more than just stories loom large. So do possibilities. "It's the backbone of Indiana trails, the longest one," Healthy Communities of Henry County's Jeff Ray said. Point your bike east and you can ride all the way to Richmond. Go the opposite direction and you could end up crossing the restaurant-laden McGalliard Road in Muncie or ride all the way to Sweetser in Grant County. Plans call for the trail to take its users much, much farther in the future.

Before it was a footpath, Cardinal Greenway moved trains across the state. Bicyclists Gerry Trout and John Dimitroff, who ironically worked together at CSX Railroad, say that they enjoy the new purpose given this former train track. "It's great recreation, and you don't have to worry about getting run over like you do sometimes on the highway," Trout said.

On this day, the duo rode to Muncie. They've also ridden the other direction, toward Richmond. Ray says there are plans in the works that could enable them to ride much farther. "Cardinal Greenway is part of the Great American Rail Trail," Ray explained. "The ultimate goal is to give users an opportunity to ride all the way to Washington, D.C. Or, if they decide to go west, to the Pacific Ocean in Washington State."

There are 3.5 miles of the trail in Henry County that opened in 2007, which coincided with Henry County's trail beginnings and its Raintree Trails Master Plan. About the same time as a $650,000 Indiana Department of Natural Resources grant landed here for the National Road Heritage Trail, another $3 million was provided to get Cardinal Greenway completed from Losantville to Richmond.

Today, Henry County has 23.5 miles of trails. Places that used to be railroad corridors are now busy with walkers, joggers and bicyclists. Blountsville resident and Healthy Communities board member Nancy Cook, who remembers when trains rolled through that part of the county, says that the transformation is well worth the state investment. "I think of all the things they could have done with this," Cook said. "The trail was the best decision they could have made."

Cook has the unique distinction of walking here when the tracks and railroad ties lined the path. She remembers walking to her office job at the former fertilizer plant. Today, she still walks the same path and enjoys the fact that it's much smoother than before. But memories reach out to her like branches of trees along the trail. "This was still a railroad when we moved out here in 1976," she said. "There was a fertilizer plant back there which was originally a Ford dealership and they brought in Model Ts. A lot of people would catch the train and go to Ball State."

Alongside colorful plants, diversified wildlife and native vegetation, legends also grow. It's been reported that a famous visitor once walked in the Blountsville vicinity where the Henry County portion of the trail begins. Not for recreation, but out of frustration.

Cook called attention to a newspaper article written a few years ago by Chris Flook, then president of the Delaware County Historical Society and currently an associate lecturer of telecommunications at Ball State University. The article, part of his "By Gone" Muncie series, reflected on a November 11, 1946 evening in which "two overwrought Englishman" were seen walking down Indiana 35.

George Kilmer, owner of Kilmer Car and Tractor Company south of Muncie, greeted them to see if he could help. He learned that one of the men was due to give a lecture at Earlham College in Richmond that evening when the vehicle's left rear wheel suddenly flew off. Fortunately, the driver was able to maintain enough control to stop the vehicle on the road's shoulder.

When Indianapolis Colts quarterback Andrew Luck was recovering from injury, he could be seen riding along the Cardinal Greenway to get back in shape. *Indianapolis Colts.*

So, Kilmer dispatched a tow truck to bring the broken-down vehicle back to his shop and then offered the man—who was to speak in Richmond that evening—a ride to Earlham College. Because his passenger was said to have a distinct English accent, Kilmer asked, perhaps in jest, if he knew famous British leader Winston Churchill. "Well, I should know him very well," the passenger replied. "I'm his son."

The passenger was none other than Randolph Churchill, as Flook described in his article, a "World War II British Army officer, former conservative member of Parliament, journalist and, yes, son of Prime Minister Winston Churchill."

Ray offered his own celebrity story about this particular trail. He said that now-retired Indianapolis Colts quarterback Andrew Luck was seen riding his bicycle on the Cardinal Greenway as he tried to bounce back from injury a few years ago. "He could ride faster here," Ray explained. "He couldn't get it done on the Monon [the Indianapolis-area trail] because it was too busy and too many people knew him. So he came up here to get more miles in."

Cardinal Greenway offers more than just relaxation and recreation. It is also a living history lesson. Along the path, a large stone-carved "W" can be seen. Ray explained that the sign, chiseled during a time before railroad warning lights and automatic signals, was a reminder to the train engineer to blow his whistle because an intersection was up ahead.

While walking along the trail, Cook pointed to a farm scene worthy of framing. She said that the picturesque area was once the farm of Miles Marshall's grandmother Julia. Marshall was publisher of the *Henry County News Republican*, a weekly newspaper in New Castle, and also served as county clerk. "When Miles's dad, Dr. Lloyd C. Marshall, was a very young boy, he would cut lumber on this farm, load it on a wagon and take it to Mount Summit," Cook said.

Stories of families past share the scenery here with animal families present. Cook said that she saw a mother mink with five little pups literally parade in front of her. She's also seen foxes and a bald eagle.

Former Blue River Valley teacher Christie Fouse said that she rides the trail "every chance I get." She was one of several bikers on this day, but the bike she rode was an interesting looking three-wheeler.

Angie Pool, chief executive officer of Cardinal Greenway Inc., offered even more perspective on the trail. "The Cardinal Greenway (CG) incorporated in 1993 when the land was purchased from CSX to build trail for all to enjoy," she said. "Cardinal Greenway Inc. owns and manages the trail system. After years of love and labor Cardinal Greenway now boasts 62 miles of paved trail spanning five East Central Indiana counties."

"It has been awarded numerous awards and earned many designations," she added. "The CG has long been designated an Indiana Visionary Trail and was designated a National Rails to Trails Conservancy Hall of Fame Trail in 2018, our 25th anniversary year. It was designated Indiana's Stakeholder Trail in 2019 for the Great American Rail Trail's route through our state."

Pool was also awarded the Outstanding Trail Leader at the 2019 International Trail Symposium. "We do not take these many awards and honors lightly," Pool said. "The staff, Board of Directors and volunteers work continuously to raise funds to work on keeping the trail in the shape our thousands of annual trail users have come to expect. We have a challenging goal but are determined to keep the trail an award-winning feature for all to enjoy. It will take all of us though, so as you enjoy our trail or any trail take a moment to give back to the organization that works so hard to keep it usable."

No, Cardinal Greenway, the granddaddy of trails, doesn't speak. He lets the birds do that for him these days. He also listens to the joyful noises, the grandfatherly talks, the determined running and pedaling as hundreds of people use the trail on a regular basis. People like Fouse and her husband, a granddad who takes grandchildren to a bridge over Stoney Creek so they can explore.

The popularity of the trail was put into perspective for Fouse recently. The woman who grew up in Blountsville said on one recent day, she passed as many as ninety people while riding her bike—young, old and every age in between. Ninety people. That's roughly 60 percent the size of Blountsville's entire population, a snapshot in time that speaks volumes for the Henry County leg of the Cardinal Greenway.

GLEN COVE CEMETERY: A LIVING HISTORY LESSON

It was a dark and stormy night when nearly forty people attended a presentation in a Knightstown cemetery on Halloween eve—not for a haunting mystery but for enduring history.

The focus was on Glen Cove—not the name of a famous person, but of a cemetery that's now the latest Henry County location to be added to the National Register of Historic Places. The final resting place of about twenty-two thousand people—and counting—is alive and well, thanks to a group of forward-thinking people who called themselves the Odd Fellows.

Bill Selm, a historian for Indianapolis Historic Preservation, an IUPUI adjunct faculty member and the author of numerous successful National Register nominations, gave an impressive three-tier lesson not only about Glen Cove and old Knightstown cemeteries, but also of the national rural cemetery movement, as well as the International Order of Odd Fellows Lodge, which played such a key role in it all.

Bill Selm is an IUPUI adjunct faculty member and author of numerous successful National Register nominations. *From the* Courier-Times.

"Glen Cove exists because of the vision of the Independent Order of Odd Fellows, Knightstown Lodge No. 99," Selm told the crowd as he shared a PowerPoint presentation. "This lodge was instituted in 1851. It was one of many lodges founded throughout Indiana and North America."

The Knightstown Lodge dissolved around 1996, and its imposing 1898 Lodge Hall—where the Alhambra Theatre was located on the ground floor—was demolished in 1992. But the efforts of Odd Fellows here will live on, ironically through the cemetery they took the lead in establishing. "Glen Cove Cemetery is the surviving legacy of this once vibrant, active institution of Knightstown," Selm said. "It is, itself, a monument to this important charitable organization."

The cemetery is not named for a person. Rather, its name comes from topography. So does the beauty that ultimately made it a candidate for the National Register. Selm said it was Odd Fellow J.E. Barrett, the local lodge's secretary, who advocated that the organization take the lead in Knightstown to provide "an adequate cemetery suitable for a community." "Barrett saw the cemetery as an opportunity for the lodge to do something worthwhile and of lasting benefit for both town and community," Selm said. "At its Dec. 14, 1886 meeting, the lodge named the cemetery Glen Cove after Glen Run, a tributary to Montgomery Creek, which is to the west."

The first burial here came in 1886, when Morris Bundy, a member of the local Odd Fellows, was laid to rest.

Glen Cove Cemetery now encompasses what is called the old Knightstown Cemetery at the south end. That cemetery, Selm explained, "was on flat ground with no impressive features." Selm said that there was a lack of planning involved and that it was unorganized. There are no records. About half of it consisted of a Baptist church graveyard. "I think it was a free-for-all," Selm said. "I think if you wanted a grave, you came up here, claimed a spot and dug a hole."

But when the Odd Fellows entered the picture, it all changed. "Glen Cove embraces and is harmonious with the irregular natural terrain," Selm said. "The old Knightstown cemetery is the resting place of the pioneer generation of Knightstown. The combined cemetery is the product of an aesthetic movement, and it possesses excellent examples of period funerary art in the form of headstones and mausolea. It is also the product of trained design professionals and landscape architects."

Many may not realize it, but Glen Cove Cemetery was designed by some of the same people involved with the well-known and respected Crown Hill Cemetery in Indianapolis. Selm said that John Chislett Jr. applied a picturesque cemetery design to Glen Cove. "At the time of his Glen Cove work, he was assistant superintendent of the renowned Crown Hill Cemetery in Indianapolis, which is also part of the National Register," Selm said. "Frederick Chislett, his grandfather, was Crown Hill's first superintendent. He was in charge of maintaining and managing the original design of Crown Hill, which was the work of his father, John Chislett Sr."

Glen Cove Cemetery is more than a place or historic site, for that matter, according to Selm. It is a living history of a movement when disposing of the dead changed. "A rational and sanitary movement to the problems with disposing of the dead began in Europe in rapidly growing cities, especially London and Paris," Selm said. "Landscape cemetery began in the U.S. at Boston in 1831. The success in Boston inspired others like Philadelphia, Baltimore, Cincinnati and Brooklyn."

Selm said that at the time, cemeteries began to serve dual purposes. In addition to being the final resting place of loved ones, they became almost like parks, where people could walk, encounter nature and remember loved ones at the same time.

Selm credited the late Tom and Peg Mayhill, newspaper publishers here over many decades, for their research and leadership in cemetery matters here. "Mr. Mayhill, God bless him, loved history so much, and he was a hands-on guy," Selm said. "He went after it. He had this intellectual curiosity and then published cemetery records for all to use. His work was important to me in my research."

Selm summed up the evening this way: "The National Register status recognizes the cultural importance of the cemetery as a product of the rural cemetery movement and of the civic and charitable work of a once very popular fraternal organization, the Odd Fellows."

As early cemetery advocate J.E. Barrett had hoped, Selm said that Glen Cove Cemetery remains "something worthwhile and of lasting benefit to the town and community" more than 133 years after it was founded.

Glen Cove Cemetery Listed in the National Register of Historic Places

For nearly three decades, Barbara Carter heard a common question at the antiques mall she and her husband owned. "People came from all over the United States and commented on how beautiful Glen Cove Cemetery looked," said Carter, vice-president of Historic Knightstown Inc. "They always asked if something special was going on in town. There were so many flowers. The chapel was so unique and the fountain was beautiful."

Carter's reply? "You know, she just looks that way all the time."

Today, the flowering praise for Glen Cove Cemetery is more than just words. Like the ornamental letters on its variety of funerary art, the significance and magnificence of the facility is now etched permanently in the National Register of Historic Places.

Carter told the story during a 2021 Memorial Day weekend ceremony to recognize Old Knightstown and Glen Cove Cemetery's inclusion in the National Register. Bright sunshine and blue skies blended with patriotic music and heartfelt remarks to celebrate the occasion. Brotherly love was beautifully expressed for the facility by Robin Richey, who performed patriotic and spiritual music on his keyboard, and younger brother Kevin Richey, who read a certificate from the International Order of Odd Fellow. "The Odd Fellows mission is to visit the sick, relieve the stressed, bury the dead and educate the orphan," Kevin read. "My past is here, your past is here, our family is here."

Sarah Ward, president of the Glen Cove Cemetery Advisory Board, presided over the Sunday program with the same passion and care that her late parents, Ralph and Susie Ward, showed for forty years. Her dad was treasurer of the cemetery, and her mother often had the task of typing up records.

When Denise Peacock and Stephanie White-Longworth unveiled the official National Register marker, its golden letters shined a light on nearly 140 years of history, the roots of which extend from the nearly twenty-two thousand people buried here to national and even international cemetery movements.

The combined cemeteries became just the fourteenth site in Henry County added to the National Register in June 2019. Since then, Henry County Memorial Park has also been added, giving the county fifteen entries on the coveted list.

But of all the county places now listed in the National Register, this one might be the most unique. Or perhaps the appropriate word is *odd*.

Historian William Selm of Indianapolis served as keynote speaker for the occasion and described in vivid detail how the International Order of Odd Fellows in Knightstown, No. 99, made it its mission to take the lead in providing "an adequate cemetery suitable for a community."

It was a common mission for Odd Fellow organizations throughout the state. Selm said that state architectural and archaeological database records show seventy-six Odd Fellow cemeteries in thirty-two of Indiana's ninety-two counties. But Glen Cove Cemetery stands out, Selm said, "as the largest with the most picturesque design and terrain of all."

"This cemetery has distinctive features—a fine collection of funerary art and its planned landscape and the Knightstown cemetery holds the graves of many of the town pioneers," Selm said. "The combined cemetery is significant in American and local history as a product of the rural cemetery movement of the 19th century. This is especially the case for Glen Cove."

"Glen Cove is the work of two professional cemetery designers," Selm continued. "The Glen Cove design embraces the natural landscape of the locale. The curved and linear paths frame the sections following the contours of the landscape. The combined cemetery expresses the changing style of the funerary art and design with its fine collection of antebellum headstones, Victorian and early 20th century monuments and mausoleum. The combined cemetery also includes four historic contributing buildings— the biggest and best one, the one right behind me, the 1915 chapel, but others include a boulder faced bridge, a cast-iron memorial fountain and monumental steel fence with matching gates."

It was Odd Fellow J.D. Barrett, then lodge secretary, who advocated that the Odd Fellows should take the lead in Knightstown to provide "an adequate cemetery suitable for a community." In 1883, the town acquired 3.5 acres of land to use as a cemetery. Barrett saw the cemetery expansion as an opportunity for the Odd Fellows to do something worthwhile and of lasting benefit to both town and community.

In 1918, another 6.5 acres were added. Today, the cemetery includes about 51 acres. The founding of Glen Cove Cemetery was a local expression of a national movement of the Odd Fellows, who were establishing cemeteries throughout the United States in the nineteenth and early twentieth centuries.

On September 30, 1887, the lodge purchased 17.5 acres immediately north and contiguous to existing public cemetery. The following month, the Odd Fellows hired John Chislett, who was at the time the assistant superintendent of the Crown Hill Cemetery in Indianapolis. "So I consider this the daughter of Crown Hill—without the Hill," Selm said. "Now Chislett, his grandfather, is the engineer who laid out Crown Hill Cemetery. Chislett's father, Frederick, was the first superintendent.

On December 14, 1886, the lodge named the cemetery Glen Cove after Glen Run. "Now he's not buried here," Selm said. "Glen Run is the creek down there, which is a tributary to Montgomery Creek."

Selm said that the first burial of this new cemetery was Odd Fellow Morris Bundy in 1886. Also among those buried here is Waitsel M. Carey, who is credited with founding Knightstown in 1827. He was the one who named the town in honor of Jonathan Knight, the engineer for the National Road that runs through the community. The remains of former residents from as far away as California, Texas and Florida have been returned for burial here.

Many over the years have helped maintain, preserve and improve the cemetery, people like late newspaper publishers and community leaders Tom and Peg Mayhill. Tom Mayhill diligently researched and published the first real cemetery records here.

From 1923 until 1996, the local Odd Fellows lodge here was in charge of the cemetery. Its members were active in raising funds to reset stones and place markers as needed. In 1996, the local lodge, with its membership aging and dwindling, transferred control back to the Town of Knightstown.

The 2021 Memorial Day program also had a distinctive patriotic feeling in the air. Pastor Tony Darling's prayer gave thanks "for those who have stormed foreign shores, flown over foreign skies, parachuted on foreign ground and sailed foreign seas…in pursuit of liberty and freedom." Pat Cronk performed stirring renditions of "The Star-Spangled Banner" and

Larry Wheat plays "Taps" during a 2021 ceremony celebrating Glen Cove Cemetery's inclusion into the National Register of Historic Places. *From the* Courier-Times.

"The Battle Hymn of Republic." Ally Piper, a youth, read the poignant World War I poem "In Flanders Fields."

A hush spread among the crowd as Larry Wheat played taps. A sense of encouraging irony also wafted through the breeze. During a ceremony for a place where more than 22,200 people are buried, it was obvious that both the Odd Fellows legacy and Knightstown community pride are indeed alive and well.

Remembering Helen Keller's Visit to New Castle

"Life is either a daring adventure, or nothing." "Alone we can do so little; together we can do so much." "The best and most beautiful things in the world cannot be seen or even touched—they must be felt with the heart."

She was a prolific author, writing fourteen books and hundreds of speeches on topics ranging from animals to Mahatma Gandhi. She traveled to thirty-five countries around the world and was America's first goodwill ambassador to Japan. She became an outspoken advocate for the rights of others, even though she struggled to speak. Her words still inspire today, even though she could not hear.

Her name was Helen Keller, and history says that she was one of the twentieth century's leading humanitarians and cofounder of the American Civil Liberties Union. While many may be aware of her incredible story, some—perhaps many—may not realize that on Tuesday, October 15, 1940, she was in New Castle.

A front-page article in the October 16, 1940 issue of the *Courier-Times* provides details of a monumental event the day before at New Castle High School, one that drew nearly 1,200 people to the Walnut Street facility.

Sponsored by the New Castle Business and Professional Women's Club, Helen Keller's appearance here gave local residents up-close-and-personal insight into one of the world's most inspiring people. Local BPW president Verena Hutson had the honor of introducing Miss Keller and her companion, Polly Thomson.

The article reported that tribute was paid to Mrs. Anne Sullivan Macy, Miss Keller's "late great teacher and who has been called responsible for the development of one of the most remarkable women of this day." Macy, who taught Keller personally over a forty-nine-year period, died on October 20, 1936, little more than four years before the twentieth-century icon visited New Castle.

Keller's remarks at the New Castle event struck both emotional and patriotic chords, according to the newspaper article. With help from Thomson, who occasionally added clarity to Keller's comments, her words no doubt riveted local residents in attendance that night.

This is part of what she said on that special night in 1940:

> *In these unprecedented days of sorrow and anxiety, blessings once sweet to us have turned to ashes because freedom in a large part of the world is at bay.*

Right: Helen Keller was sixty years old when she gave a presentation in New Castle. *Wikimedia Commons.*

Below: Helen Keller's October 15, 1940 visit made front-page news in the *Courier-Times.*

But however dark things may be, we have the light of faith at our command. Faith is a brave search for new paths to life; faith is a white fire of enthusiasm, a mental perception of what is good.

Only by clinging resolutely to faith can we choose a way of life and contribute our talents to civilization.

Americans, for the most part, had not had faith enough in themselves to keep democracy constructive. They have shirked responsibilities and faith has been left to preachers and dreamers.

We cannot long evade an answer to the cynical and pessimistic doctrine that force, not human betterment, is the world's ideal. We dare not run the risk of revival of barbarism and the mutilation of mankind by war and intolerance.

The founders of this nation made faith, by example, a vital duty.

Moved by these stabbing issues, we must help roll back this flood of evil ideals with the faith of Lexington and Concord, the faith which has emancipated the human mind, the faith which looks beyond all discouragement to a remade world in which the flame of liberty and decency burns steady and unconsumed.

Her words then seem prophetic now. Little more than a year after she spoke in New Castle, the Japanese bombed Pearl Harbor and America was thrust into World War II and a titanic struggle between good and evil.

An Amazing Life

Helen Keller's amazing life was all about "looking beyond all discouragement." Biographers say that Helen, an Alabama native and daughter of a Confederate army officer, was born with senses of sight and hearing, but disease took them away before she was two years old. History tells us that she was just nineteen months of age when stricken with an illness the family doctor called "brain fever" that produced a high body temperature. In the many years that have passed, some doctors have speculated that Helen's disease might have been scarlet fever or meningitis.

As Helen grew into childhood, she developed a limited method of communication with her companion, Martha Washington, the young daughter of the family cook. The two had created a type of sign language. By the time Helen was seven, they had invented more than sixty signs to communicate with each other.

Yet if some family members had prevailed, Helen Keller would have been institutionalized. Biographers wrote that Keller became very wild and unruly. She would kick and scream when angry and giggle uncontrollably when happy. She tormented Martha and inflicted raging tantrums on her parents.

Had she been institutionalized, Helen Keller would not have become the worldwide inspiration who visited New Castle in 1940.

Finding Answers

Three classic names—Charles Dickens, Alexander Graham Bell and Mark Twain—are also part of Helen's incredible story.

Looking for answers and inspiration, Keller's mother came across a travelogue by Charles Dickens, *American Notes*, in 1886. She read of the successful education of another deaf and blind child, Laura Bridgman, and soon dispatched Keller and her father to Baltimore, Maryland, to see specialist Dr. J. Julian Chisolm.

After examining Keller, Chisolm recommended that she see Alexander Graham Bell, the inventor of the telephone, who was working with deaf children at the time. Bell met with Keller and her parents and suggested that they travel to the Perkins Institute for the Blind in Boston, Massachusetts.

There, the family met with the school's director, Michael Anaganos. He suggested that Keller work with one of the institute's most recent graduates, a woman named Anne Sullivan.

On March 3, 1887, Sullivan went to Keller's home in Alabama and immediately went to work. She began by teaching six-year-old Keller finger spelling, starting with the word *doll*, to help Keller understand the gift of a doll she had brought along. Other words would follow.

At first, Keller was curious, then defiant, refusing to cooperate with Sullivan's instruction. When Keller did cooperate, Sullivan could tell that she wasn't making the connection between the objects and the letters spelled out in her hand. Sullivan kept working at it, forcing Keller to go through the regimen.

As Keller's frustration grew, the tantrums increased. Finally, Sullivan demanded that she and Keller be isolated from the rest of the family for a time so that Keller could concentrate only on Sullivan's instruction. They moved to a cottage on the plantation.

In a dramatic struggle, Sullivan taught Keller the word *water*. She helped her make the connection between the object and the letters by taking Keller out to the water pump and placing Keller's hand under the spout. While Sullivan moved the lever to flush cool water over Keller's hand, she spelled out the word *w-a-t-e-r* on Keller's other hand. Keller understood and repeated the word in Sullivan's hand. She then pounded the ground, demanding to know its "letter name." Sullivan followed her, spelling out the word into her hand. Keller moved to other objects with Sullivan in tow. By nightfall, she had learned thirty words.

Keller worked with Anne Sullivan for forty-nine years, from 1887 until Sullivan's death in 1936. In 1932, Sullivan experienced health problems and lost her eyesight completely. A young woman named Polly Thomson, who had begun working as a secretary for Keller and Sullivan in 1914, became Keller's constant companion upon Sullivan's death. Polly was the one who accompanied Helen to New Castle in 1940.

Helen Praises School Band

The *Courier-Times* article on Helen Keller's appearance here noted that she "congratulated the high school orchestra directed by Carroll Copeland, which played for the program, and said she enjoyed music, and even dancing when she 'had a good partner.'" The article also reported that a reception was held for Keller at the Plaza Hotel before the event.

As her story became known to the general public, Keller began to meet famous and influential people. One of them was the writer Mark Twain, who was very impressed with her. They became friends.

Like Twain, Helen Keller was also a wordsmith. Her inspirational quotes dot the Information Superhighway, more than five decades after her death on June 1, 1968. Eighty-one years after she was a guest of the New Castle BPW, one of her quotes still speaks loudly to all who would hear: "Keep your face to the sunshine and you cannot see the shadows."

FAMED POET PUTS DECORATION DAY IN BRILLIANT PERSPECTIVE

Deep, tender, warm and true, a nation's heart
Throbs for the brave ones that have passed away
Who, in Grim Battle's drama played their part,
And slumber here today.

So began a moving military tribute written by a man who became known as the "Hoosier Poet," James Whitcomb Riley. It was May 30, 1876, and Riley, then just twenty-six years old, had written the poem especially for the New Castle Decoration Day ceremony at South Mound Cemetery.

Riley and New Castle's own poet laureate, Benjamin Parker, were good friends. Parker called him "a young man of decided genius."

The original poem, titled "A Different Thing to Do," puts our modern Memorial Day observances into perspective, even though the words were written well over a century ago.

Some misunderstandings about Memorial Day still exist. It is not a day to honor all veterans. That day comes on November 11. It is a time intended to reflect and appreciate those who gave their lives in military service, a day to honor those who did not come back from battle.

Riley's poem puts the occasion and the ultimate sacrifice given by so many into eloquent perspective:

> *When angry guns, like famished beasts of prey*
> *Were howling for their gory feast of lives,*
> *And sending dismal echoes far away*
> *To mothers and to wives.*
> *The mother, kneeling in the empty night,*
> *With pleading hands uplifted for the son*
> *Who, even as she prayed, had fought the fight—*
> *The victory had been won.*
> *The wife—with trembling hand that wrote to say,*
> *The babe was waiting for the sire's caress*
> *The letter meeting that upon the way—*
> *The babe was fatherless.*
> *And lives that bound themselves in strongest chain*
> *Are sundered and the broken links of love*
> *In fragments now, must evermore remain*
> *Until rejoined above.*

Since that Memorial Day 1876 occasion in South Mound Cemetery, many more Henry County mothers, wives, fathers, brothers, sisters, sons and daughters have experienced firsthand the emotions Riley described in his poem. Just forty-one years after that event, the United States entered World War I, when at least twenty-five county residents gave their lives.

Left: James Whitcomb Riley, who became known as the "Hoosier Poet" during his lifetime, became close friends with New Castle's own poet laureate, Benjamin Parker. *Wikimedia Commons*.

Right: Benjamin Parker—writer, newspaper editor, lawyer and legislator—was a close friend of James Whitcomb Riley. *Henry County Historical Society*.

A mere twenty-four years after that, World War II came, and many brave Henry County residents went, with forty-four soldiers never making it back home to enjoy the freedom they fought so hard to preserve.

Just eleven years later, duty called again and Henry County answered, bravely taking the fight against Communism to Korea. Today, there are twenty-two names etched in their honor, those who paid the ultimate price in defense of their nation.

After another eleven years passed, young Henry Countians were faced with the horrors of war once again, this time in Vietnam. Names of nineteen soldiers killed in another war so very far away are etched in gray at Memorial Park.

Then came Operation Desert Storm in 1991 and the War on Terror in 2001. Henry County paid the price and made the sacrifice in those military encounters, too, in Afghanistan and Iraq.

Each Memorial Day weekend, they should be more than just names on a wall. We may not have met them, yet we knew them all.

Many of them loved to stand on a green hill, in a place like Memorial Park, look over the landscape below, breathe in the fresh air and literally taste the freedom—just like us.

Many of them loved to hear the laughter of children as they played in a safe place, unafraid of what enemy could be lurking over the hill.

Many of them loved to look at a starry night sky and dream of the possibilities their future held, a night sky not blurred by the rocket's red glare—just like us.

And so many of them gave up all the blessings we cherish—trading the green hill for a bunker, the laughter of children for the thunder of gunfire, the starry night sky for the shadows of death.

How many bedtime stories and birthday parties did they miss? How many Sunday picnics and baseball games and county fairs went on without them?

How many precious moments with loved ones were traded for the duty that makes them all possible for us today?

This is not to say that Henry County residents shouldn't enjoy the three-day Memorial Day weekend. On the contrary. The brave soldiers no longer with us wouldn't have it any other way. It's why they did what they did.

In his poem, Riley colors the somber hues with distinctive red, white and blue:

O mother, you who miss the happy face
Of that dear boy who vanished from your sight
And left you weeping o'er that vacant place
He used to fill at night.
Be glad and proud you had a life to give
Be comforted through all the years to come
Your country has a longer life to live
Your son a better home

O, widow weeping o'er the wondering child
Who lifts his questioning eyes to only send
A keener pang of grief unreconciled
Teach him to comprehend
He had a father brave enough to stand
Before the fire of Treason's blazing sun
That dying, he might will the rich old land
Of Freedom to his son
And maiden—living on thro' lonely years

In fealty to love's enduring ties
With strong faith gleaming through the tender tears
That gather in your eyes
Look up, and down in gratefulness of prayers
Submission to the will of heaven's high host
I see your angel soldier pacing there
Expectant at his post.

Military

Revolutionary War Soldier Who Stood "30 Steps from Gen. George Washington" Buried in Henry County

He served with the "Culpeper Minute Men," survived the bitter cold at Valley Forge and "stood thirty steps from Gen. George Washington" when Cornwallis surrendered at Yorktown. Christopher Long was part of the American Revolution that we celebrate each Fourth of July. Today, he's buried in Henry County, about four and a half miles east of New Castle in a most appropriate place: Liberty Township.

Long's story connects the county with the very founding of the nation. A marble monument, standing nine feet, six inches high and surrounded by an iron railing, serves as an appropriate reminder of the effort it took to win freedom for this new place called America. It is worth remembering each Fourth of July.

One writer called the Long burial site, located at County Roads 500 West and 200 South, "one of the most unique cemeteries" he'd ever seen. It didn't used to be that way. According to a story written for the *Courier-Times* by Eldon Pitts in November 2002, a traffic accident had toppled the monument and broken it into two pieces. After Pitts wrote that story, the late Bud Bush and Kenny Hartman, local history enthusiasts, restored the monument. At the time, Hartman was the county highway superintendent. Two others, Greg Brown and Chad Lawson, helped clean the monument, perhaps for the first time since a grandson of Long's had installed it in 1877.

A Washington Monument–styled obelisk rises off a rural New Castle road honoring the memory of Revolutionary War soldier Christopher Long. *From the* Courier-Times.

Former Henry County Historical Society Museum curator Marianne Hughes said that a granddaughter of Long's once visited the site and "could not believe" that any desecration had occurred. It has been considered hallowed ground for decades.

Long's story is interesting in many ways. His father, Ware Long, lived to be 112 years old. He came to America not by choice, but by exile. According to the Genealogy of Ware Long of Culpeper website, Long came here with more than one thousand other offenders due to "some political offense against the government of England."

Long was the third of twelve children, born in May 1746. The genealogy stated, "This was a tall, well-built, large-boned, muscular family, full of fight, afraid of nothing and as roving as the Arabs. They were of great stature, which was an inheritance from their father."

It wasn't just Long who entered the Revolutionary War. His five brothers also enlisted. Christopher Long was with the Virginia militia throughout the entire war. His unit was known as the "Culpeper Minute Men," and its flag featured a coiled rattlesnake preparing to spring along with the ominous warning "Don't Tread on Me." The genealogy stated that this flag was one of twelve displayed in the American army before the "Stars and Stripes" flag was finally adopted.

Long was in historic company. According to the genealogy, one of the lieutenants he served with was a young John Marshall, who afterward went on to become the longest-service Supreme Court chief justice in U.S. history, serving from 1801 to 1835.

But the most famous name Long served with was George Washington. The genealogy said, "We do know that Christopher was with Washington during his memorable campaign through the Jerseys and around Philadelphia, and that he spent the dreadful winter of 1777 and 1778 with the American Army at Valley Forge, when shivering together in their huts, they spent the nights in trying to get warm, rather than in sleep, and many a ragged soldier made it possible to follow his trail by the blood stains his naked feet left in the snow."

Long was there when the Siege of Yorktown took place in October 1781. It was the last major battle of the Revolutionary War. The genealogy noted, "When relating the events of each day of the siege of Yorktown, Long took special delight in telling that he stood thirty steps from General Washington and saw Cornwallis's sword surrendered."

Long's story has an interesting footnote after his death in 1829 at the age of eighty-three. The graves of he and his wife, Sarah, were directly in the path of a new road planned for the area. "Had it not been for the intercession of old friends, the two little mounds of earth would have been obliterated," the Long genealogy said. "However, popular opinion prevailed and a curve was made in the highway."

As Henry County prepares to observe another Fourth of July with fireworks and family gatherings, it would indeed be appropriate to take a minute and remember the Culpeper Minute Men, especially Christopher Long, who enjoyed his last years in Henry County, a place named for Patrick Henry, the man who famously said, "Give me liberty or give me death."

General William Grose Was Where Civil War "Bullets Flew the Thickest"

"This old gray-headed man here is an inspiration to the citizens of New Castle and every citizen in Henry County. How many communities can boast of such a grand old man as your old commander?"

Henry County judge Eugene Bundy pointed to the person beside him, General William Grose, at the thirteenth reunion of the Union army's 36th Regiment during the Civil War. Grose was in his twilight years on that occasion but still had that leadership sparkle.

"I do not over-estimate or over-state when I say that the war produced no braver or greater soldier than your old commander," Bundy continued. "He is an inspiration to every young man, every old man, and to everyone that lives in the community and to everyone who knows him. His career has been one of the grandest and if he should die tomorrow, he would die the honored and respected friend of all the community."

Grose was a soldier through and through. It was in his DNA. For many years—even generations—the Grose name symbolized patriotism, leadership and courage. Both of his grandfathers had served in the Revolutionary War, and one of them actually died trying to give America its first taste of freedom. His father was a soldier during the War of 1812—the war that broke the bondage with England for good and produced our national anthem in the process.

When the Civil War threatened the very existence of the nation, Grose boldly stepped forward to lead. He was there at Lookout Mountain, Chickamauga, Shiloh and Atlanta in the Civil War, helping lead the Union charge. One historian said that Grose always seemed to be "where the bullets flew the thickest." On two occasions, his horse was shot out from under him. Some war injuries were with him up until the day he died.

The names of commanders he served under reads like a PBS documentary—Don Carlos Buell, William "Bull" Nelson, George Henry Thomas and William Tecumseh Sherman. But Grose had an equally high respect for his troops. On June 6, 1885, when he relinquished command of his regiment, he is quoted as saying, "Take home and into the future with you the heartfelt gratitude of your humble commander for his lot having been cast with such valiant soldiers and kind-hearted gentlemen."

Back home in New Castle, citizens didn't have to look for or wonder where Grose was—they could hear him coming. The sound of a galloping

This 1885 stereograph of Henry County Bar Association members shows General William Grose (*on the first step at far right*). *Doug Magers.*

horse was frequently accompanied by someone yelling, "Look out, here comes Gen. Grose." It apparently was a common occurrence. Even in his later years, the general was known to live life at a brisk pace. "If you were a resident of New Castle in the 19th century, you undoubtedly were cautioned on occasion while walking the streets of New Castle to

Here's a photo of General William Grose from the 1860s. Historians wrote that General Grose was "where the bullets flew the thickest" during the Civil War. *Henry County Historical Society.*

move aside a bit while a militant gentleman on a galloping horse charged down the streets, splattering mud on passersby during rainy days or stirring up billowing clouds of dust during the droughts of summer and autumn," read an essay on Grose's life from Henry County Historical Society archives.

One interesting story about General Grose came with his faithful horse, which seemed to display the same attention to command his soldiers were known for through his military years. "Gen. Grose almost always is associated with a horse," the historical society archives said. "A horse he supposedly brought home he called 'Framey' because it was so thin. Although Framey had been wounded during the war, he still served the general faithfully and the master and the horse were very close....Now the general, we are told, was one of those methodical creatures who kept a rigid schedule. One day when time came for Framey to carry his master home from the office, the general did not appear. It was time to go, so

Framey went—stopping at the post office and the store for the customary loaf of bread, then ambling on home." Without his master.

There was no report on how General Grose got home that day. Was he angry that the horse had left him behind? Or was he smiling because the time-sensitive horse had shown such discipline and attention to schedule? Perhaps a little of both. Grose certainly knew how to get things done.

It could be argued that Grose helped New Castle grow from a small wilderness town to a thriving industrial center. "In 1848, when the railroad boom was beginning throughout the Midwest, Grose was an active participant in local meetings to bring railroad service to New Castle," historians wrote. "Three years later, the laying of tracks from Richmond to this city was underway."

In the years following railroad development here, even Grose himself seemed amazed at the rapid growth. "If you had told me when I was a boy in Fayette County that today we would see 30 passenger trains depart from New Castle daily, I would have said you were a lunatic," Grose was quoted as saying in his later years.

Anyone today who drives on Dublin Pike today also has Grose to thank. "In 1852, Grose was elected president of a company to build a turnpike or plank road from Dublin to New Castle," historians wrote. "And when the need for a machine and foundry shop became apparent in 1870, Grose put his stamp of approval on the project by saying he had a lively interest in anything that would improve the town."

He served his fellow citizens in a variety of roles away from the battlefield— as New Lisbon's postmaster, then later as a New Castle attorney and in the Indiana General Assembly, both in the House and the Senate.

General Grose was also there when the very roots of the national "Grand Old Party" were planted. In the spring of 1856, Grose attended the Pittsburg convention that organized the Republican Party and, as the local newspaper said, "had the high honor of being one of the founders of the greatest and most successful political party of modern times."

In addition to the inspiration left behind in books, photos and papers, Grose's legacy is also ever-present at 606 South 14th Street in New Castle, where his home continues to be carefully preserved by the Henry County Historical Society. Home to the Historical Society Museum since 1902, it is the oldest continuously operating facility of its kind in Indiana.

It was a late Monday afternoon when this beloved New Castle soldier fought his last battle. General Grose died on July 30, 1900, at his home on South 14th Street in New Castle. "Universal grief" was the description one

Right: A painting of General William Grose hangs in his 606 South 14th Street New Castle home. *Henry County Historical Society*.

Opposite: The stately home of General William Grose on South 14th Street in New Castle has been site of the Henry County Historical Society since 1902. *Gene Ingram*.

report used as word spread that the general was gone. The impact was felt not just in New Castle, according to the *New Castle Courier*:

> *There are very few of the older families in Henry, Delaware, Wayne, Fayette and Union counties that are not strongly attached to William Grose with the bonds of tender memories of brave boys whom they sent out with him and who shared his hardships and perils with him, willingly sacrificing their lives or returning with him at the close of the war, broken in health, to mourn the rest of their days over the wrecks of their once vigorous manhood.*
>
> *Because of these tenderest of all associations, the death of General Grose casts the deep gloom of mourning over the people of this whole section of the State as well as over multitudes farther away. And in the community which held him dear, this grief is most keen.*

The newspaper reported Grose's health had been "poor for a long time." A few days before he died, Grose suffered a second stroke of paralysis. Interestingly, however, the general was seen two or three months earlier on his horse in the downtown area. "He came through the streets on horseback, sitting as straight as an arrow and looking every inch the soldier he was," the *Courier* reported. "General Grose was known and loved by every man, woman and child in New Castle."

Just a short time after that appearance, the general was gone. His death not only made headline news but also took up most of the front page in some publications. His funeral service was reported to one of the largest in New Castle history. Since 1902, his stately home at 606 South 14th Street in New Castle has been site of the Henry County Historical Society.

A tribute to General Grose, typed in red ink on plain newsprint, is part of the historical society archives. It indicates that the galloping horse was a symbol of his life. "It wasn't necessarily true that the General's haste meant he was on a life-or-death errand," the essay read. "More likely, he was headed for his downtown office, where he practiced successfully the profession of law. Or perhaps he was on his way to the post office to get the day's mail. Maybe he was headed for the country to check on things at his farm, just west of the county poor farm."

It continued, "But this was the way William Grose did things—if he were alive today, he would be called a go-getter, a spark plug, a member of the lively generation. Energy and ambition—these attributes Grose possessed in abundance."

Somewhat poetically, General Grose, who fought hard for President Abraham Lincoln's Union army during the Civil War, died at the age of eighty-seven, which is, to borrow a phrase from the nation's sixteenth president, "four score and seven years."

A GRIEVING FATHER RETRIEVES HIS FALLEN SON'S BODY FROM A MASS GRAVE AND BRINGS HIM HOME

This is a Father's Day story. A true story that has nothing to do with children celebrating their dad and everything to do with the power of a father's love for his son. A true story that began in New Castle, traveled to the Tennessee-Georgia border—not once, but twice—and came to a solemn but victorious end at South Mound Cemetery.

Historians now agree that 750,000 people died in the Civil War. Despite the fact that Henry County was in a state where few Civil War bullets flew, its soldiers contributed to the valor, with more than 2,000 sent into battle. The late Tim Morris wrote that New Castle and Knightstown soldiers carried their rifles and bedrolls six times across Tennessee and three times across Kentucky.

Orlistus Powell did something that aggravated his father but which later was an important factor in finding his body following the bloody Battle of Chickamauga. *Henry County Historical Society.*

Five hundred of them never made it home. One of those men was Orlistus Powell. The story begins on July 11, 1861, when Henry Powell—son of local teacher, banker and politician Simon T. Powell—was injured in the Battle of Rich Mountain. He had received a severe wound to his right ankle, breaking the bone and disabling him for life. Early Henry County historian George Hazzard said that Henry Powell was the first citizen of New Castle to suffer an injury in a Civil War battle.

Henry Powell dropped everything to serve his country and, even after the debilitating injury, joined his father in encouraging enlistments, soliciting and forwarding supplies and caring for women and children of soldiers.

The Powells were so dedicated to the cause that, according to Hazzard, after Henry's injury, his younger brother, Orlistus, volunteered to serve in what became Company C of the 36th Indiana Infantry. He was a dedicated soldier, rising in rank to commissary sergeant and then sergeant major.

In a letter found within the archives of the Henry County Historical Society, Simon T. Powell had this to say about Orlistus's actions to take up the Union cause for his injured brother:

> *I was so proud of you; how you enlisted in the 36th after your brother came home from that early battle at Rich Mountain in West Virginia; the first Henry County boy wounded in this War of the Rebellion. Henry was hurt too badly to return, but you didn't hesitate. Your mother Elizabeth was proud, too, but I know she had a mother's qualms, especially for you, Orlistus; her youngest son—a man at 25 but still a boy to her—off to face the unknown terror of war.*
>
> *And the battles you fought: Perryville, Ky.; Corinth, Miss.; Shiloh, Stone's River and Tullahoma in Tennessee. Places we'd never heard of before and now will never forget. And the final one—this place with an Indian name—Chickamauga. Even the Redmen called it a "river of death"—such pathetic irony!*

On September 20, 1863, Orlistus Powell was killed in the bloody battle of Chickamauga, Georgia, a battle that produced the second-highest number of casualties, trailing only Gettysburg.

Hazzard's *History of Henry County* said that Powell's remains fell into the hands of Confederate troops, and he was buried on the battlefield. But the grieving father could not stand the thought of his son's final resting place being in a mass grave.

So Simon T. Powell left New Castle en route to Chickamauga to search for his son's body and bring him home. "Nearly four months afterward, his remains, identified under as curious a circumstance as ever came to the attention of the author, were recovered, brought home and re-interred Feb. 3, 1864, in South Mound Cemetery, New Castle," Hazzard wrote. "After the battle of Missionary Ridge, when the Federal army again occupied the old battlefield at Chickamauga, Simon T. Powell appeared on the scene to recover the body of his son, Orlistus."

"Never in my wildest imagining did I think it would come to this. That I, Simon Powell, merchant, farmer, successful in life, would be making this journey," the grieving father wrote. "After all, a father's not supposed to outlive his children, is he? God give me strength to make it through this day.…I thought Indiana winters were cold, but this damp Southern air chills my very soul. I pray the weather at least, was better for you last September here, at the place of your death. Your Captain wrote how valiant you were, but we knew that, your mother and I."

But how do you find someone in mass grave? "He was buried in a trench containing more than a dozen other bodies, thrown in promiscuously, as was the custom in both armies when burying the enemy's dead on the battlefield," Hazzard wrote of Orlistus Powell. "When young Powell was thrown in, his arm became extended horizontally at full length, with another deceased soldier's body covering it."

But on Orlistus Powell's arm was something special, something that originally irritated his father but now became a Godsend. "Do you know what my son did?" Simon T. Powell wrote. "The crazy things boys will do! He had initials tattooed—yes, tattooed—in India ink on his arm! My father would have whooped me good if I had done such a thing! Another irony— that's how we found you, son. When the Rebels laid you in this mass grave, a comrade's body fell over that arm. Do you know, we could still read those initials O.W.P.?"

Hazard wrote, "And in the first trench opened, in taking out the bodies, mangled and decomposed beyond recognition, it was found that the body resting on the arm of Orlistus had preserved, as clear and distinct as in life, the name 'O.W.P.,' thus the identification was complete and his mortal remains restored to the care of the family whose sacrifice he had been to the cause," Hazzard wrote.

Today, because of a father's love, the remains of Orlistus Powell are buried here in New Castle, nearly five hundred miles from where he died in battle—with those of his family beside him. "I've come to take you home

Thanks to his father's determination, Orlistus Powell, once buried in a mass grave, is now buried at New Castle's South Mound Cemetery. *From the* Courier-Times.

now, son," Simon T. Powell wrote. "To lay you to rest where you grew up. I know you'll miss your comrades here, but we need you close to us. Your mother, especially. A man's strong, after all, but women grieve differently, don't they? You'll be in that fine cemetery at South Mound. Remember that peaceful place not far from your own home? We used to go there for picnics. We'll put up a fine POWELL marker there and all be together for our last, peaceful rest."

"Well, it's time to board the train back home," Simon Powell's letter concluded. "I wish you were sitting here beside me. I wish I could have taken your place. I wish.…But wishes are pointless, aren't they? All we can do is what we have to do and live with our memories. You'll live with us forever, son, but how we will miss you!"

Paintings of both Simon T. Powell and his son Orlistus hang in the Henry County Historical Society museum today. In fact, the elder Powell's painting was one of the first given to the museum.

New Castle's General Omar Bundy: How Disobeying an Order Saved Paris from the Germans

Born in New Castle about two months after the Civil War started, it seemed that Omar Bundy was destined for military greatness.

A look into *Courier-Times* news clippings reaffirms just how heroic Bundy really was. The impact he had on the outcome of World War I is significant, not just according to news clippings from his hometown paper but also in photos showing him with General John J. Pershing and President Franklin D. Roosevelt. His medals included not only the U.S. Army's Silver Star but also the Legion of Honor and Croix de Guerre with Palms from France, praising him for "the stubborn defense and obstinate counterattacks" that helped stop the German offensive before Chateau Thierry.

It was, according to a Monday, January 22, 1940 *Courier-Times* newspaper article on Bundy's life, one of two moments where he displayed monumental leadership. "Two brilliant instances of his leadership occurred in late May, 1918, when the rush of his division stemmed the German advance at Chateau Thierry and July 15 when his famous counter attack resulted in the first great allied victory," the article reported.

The second of those, known as the Battle of Belleau Wood, is regarded by some sources as a turning point for the United States in World War I. And it all started when Bundy disobeyed an order. "Belleau Wood had been

General Omar Bundy, a New Castle native, led troops in the Battle of Belleau Wood during World War I. He refused an order to retreat, a move historians say in all probability saved Paris from capture by the Germans. *Henry County Historical Society.*

held by the Germans for months and the fact that repeated Allied efforts to drive the Germans from their trenches in the woods had utterly failed made Belleau Wood not only a military objective of importance to the allies but a mental bogey which had many Allied leaders doubting they could take it," the archived article said. "The Germans had boasted that they couldn't be driven from this position."

"On July 15, he [Bundy] was second in command of the American second division and other allied troops near Belleau Wood, just a few miles from the town of Chateau Thierry. Early in the morning when the Germans thought the French would be heavy from the effects of Bastille Day, the Germans opened a vicious attack. Preceded by gas and high explosive bombardment, the German shock troops came on in waves against the Franco-American lines. As usual in these fiendish battering-ram attacks, the line bent."

"The indomitable but wearying Poilus [French infantry] gave ground in the face of overwhelming numbers and superior artillery," the archived article continued. "All the world looked with hopeless eyes upon the possibility of a new wedge being driven in the line that might carry the Hun host to the outskirts of Paris."

"It was in the face of this attack that General Bundy refused the order of his French superior to retreat and ordered the famous counter attack," the 1940 *Courier-Times* newspaper article concluded.

Bundy responded to his French superior's order with this now iconic statement: "We regret being unable to follow the counsels of our masters, the French, but the American flag has been compelled to retire. This is unendurable and none of our soldiers would understand not being asked to do whatever is necessary to reestablish a situation which is humiliating to us and unacceptable to our country's honor. We are going to counter attack."

Bundy's counterattack not only stopped the German advance, but it also enabled the Allied forces to drive the Germans entirely out of Belleau Wood. "It was the first great Allied victory, it marked the taking of a primary military objective and it gave heart and courage to the entire Allied forces. As the result of this great success, General Bundy became famed as the 'hero of Belleau Wood.'"

It was a signature triumph for a New Castle native who had already made other military marks. Bundy also fought against the Sioux Indians in South Dakota in 1890–91 and was with General John J. Pershing on the Mexican border.

"New Castle was brought to the full realization today that the Rose City is the home of one whose great achievements turned the world's war for democracy from one of victory for imperialism to an utter rout and ultimate defeat," one newspaper article described. "Older residents of the village of 3,000 inhabitants where Major-General Omar Bundy was born and spent his early life have known him as an old-time friend and through the years past have kept in touch with his record as an officer in the U.S. Army, but few of the present 16,000 residents of the now city of Newcastle knew of General Bundy until he became the hero of Chateau-Thierry."

Bundy Auditorium in New Castle has been site for many musical, dramatic and special events since opening in the 1972. The auditorium, made possible by generous donations from General Omar Bundy and his wife, Addie, was renovated in 2023. *From the* Courier-Times.

Reports indicated, however, that General Bundy was more interested in his sister's cooking than being celebrated in a parade. "Major Gen. Bundy disdains a fuss over himself," a newspaper article said. "Those who know him declare that he shuns the limelight, but nevertheless is a jolly good fellow and all soldier. Major Gen. Bundy is promised some old-fashioned pumpkin pies by his sister, Mrs. David W. Chambers, and some fresh Indiana bass when he arrives."

For many years, New Castle residents have enjoyed two impressive reminders of Bundy's heroism and generosity. Bundy Auditorium, built with money donated by the general and his wife, Addie, has served the community for decades. Also, a German cannon at Henry County Memorial Park taken by Bundy in his heroic battles has been a focal point for generations of youth who have climbed and sat atop it.

One other reminder of Bundy's significance in not just local but national history can be found in Washington, D.C. The New Castle native is buried alongside his wife at Arlington National Cemetery. General Omar Bundy was a World War I hero.

New Castle's General Omar Bundy Leaves a Twenty-Thousand-Pound Reminder of His Bravery

Anyone who thinks that small can't become mighty needs to look at the top of a Memorial Park hill. There sits a German cannon weighing nearly twenty thousand pounds. A short distance down that hill, a new monument tells the story of how a five-foot, five-inch-tall man led American forces in capturing it.

Sunny skies and an air of freedom blew gently during the dedication of a new memorial honoring New Castle native Omar Bundy. About one hundred people were on hand to see the unveiling, learn about General Bundy and be reminded that anything is possible—even in a small town. "I think if Gen. Bundy was here, he'd have a smile on his face," speaker Wayne Graham said.

Bundy would have been particularly impressed with how the museum-quality monument came to be that features his image, his story and a map of where he served during World War I. His great-great-niece, Virginia Chambers Reeves, a key member of the family who founded the *Courier-Times*, was the driving force in making it all happen. "This has been a dream of mine," she said after the official unveiling.

Memorial Park superintendent Laurie Davis stands next to Virginia Chambers during the unveiling of a monument dedicated to General Omar Bundy. Chambers, part of a family who created the *Courier-Times*, provided the funds for the monument. *From the* Courier-Times.

Memorial Park Board president Landon Dean joined many others in expressing appreciation to Reeves for being the driving financial and historical force in making the monument a reality. "When you wrote that letter about your project idea to the board, I knew it would be nice," Dean said. "But I never envisioned anything like this. It's absolutely beautiful."

Aileen McGrady, widow of longtime Memorial Park superintendent and World War II veteran John McGrady, was asked what her late husband would think of the newest addition to the place he loved. "Oh my gosh— wouldn't that be something. John would be proud of this," she said.

Graham read many names as he credited those who worked so hard on the monumental addition, from park employees Gary Whittle and Terry Ewing to County Highway superintendent Joe Wiley and his crew, GEO and IMI officials, local elected leaders, Mike Modjeski of Miller-Wearly Monuments, Abbott's Tree Service, McGrady Outdoors, Ameriturf, Whitaker Concrete and Monument Restoration, Ron Gossage and many others.

Graham said that the driving forces behind the monument—much in the same vein as Bundy's determined soldiers—were two women: Reeves and Memorial Park superintendent Laurie Davis. "You know when two women get their heads together, something is going to happen," Graham said.

Even though Reeves now winters in Florida, Graham said that the project built up steam like a locomotive all the way to its conclusion. He joked that if cellphones didn't exist and long-distance phone charges were still common, "Ma Bell would have been a rich person" with all the calls made between Reeves and Davis.

In his remarks, a second speaker, A.J. Vulgan, a good friend of Reeves, said that there remains great symbolism in what General Bundy did in World War I and what citizens of his hometown can do today. He wove General Bundy's famous refusal to retreat during a key battle in France into his remarks but also tied in the efforts of Moina Belle Michael, a Georgia woman history now regards as the "Poppy Lady."

She was inspired by an opening line in a John McCrae battlefront poem "In Flanders Fields":

> *In Flanders fields the poppies blow*
> *Between the crosses row on row.*

Michael made it her mission to help support and honor American soldiers by wearing a red poppy as symbol of remembrance for those who served in the war and raised money with red poppy sales to help both veterans and their families.

On this particular Sunday, in addition to the unveiling of General Bundy's monument in Memorial Park, red poppies could be found under a nearby tree. While they were artificial, Superintendent Davis said that real ones would be planted, accenting the Bundy Memorial and reminding everyone of the great sacrifices made during World War I along with all the battles that have followed.

Vulgan said that both Bundy and Michael had another commonality in addition to their World War I efforts: "There was a man from a small town in Indiana and a woman from a small town in Georgia who had a big impact on this world. They remind us how we, too, can have an impact. It's important for us to understand that no matter how big or small the giving is, it can be like that proverbial stone that breaks the surface of the pond and each ripple grows out from it."

Rescuing a Cannon

Up the hill from the "monument-al" tribute to Bundy is the twenty-thousand-pound German Krupp cannon captured by his forces in the Battle of Belleau Wood. It was first placed on the Memorial Park perch in 1926. Indiana's weather took a heavy toll on the artillery piece over the years. Several of the spokes on the metal wheels rusted through, and oxidation of other wheel parts as well as the cannon itself necessitated a major overhaul.

The cannon's condition was noticed when the Walter P. Chrysler High School class of 1966 met to continue a reunion tradition—climbing on and posing around the cannon for a photo. One of its members, Gene Ingram, also happened to be president of the Henry County Historical Society. After the picture, he took a closer look at the cannon. What he found was equal to General Bundy's famous words—"unendurable" and "unacceptable" to what the cannon had stood for all these years.

On a March day in 2014, Randy Neal along with his son, Scott, used equipment from their business to lift and transport the twenty-thousand-pound cannon off the Memorial Park hill and to Neal's Scrap Metal for initial repair work. For the first time in eighty-eight years, the hilltop stood alone after Ingram had received permission from the Henry County commissioners to "steal the cannon" for a while.

"We took it to Randy's place at first because it was still warm weather," Ingram recalled. "We started disassembling it and it was in even worse shape than we actually thought."

When cold weather descended, the cannon was taken to Magna Machine and Tool near Messick. "We got it inside for a few months at Magna," Ingram said. "Kirk Robbins, Doug Hinshaw and Bruce Schmidt, the co-owners, were kind enough to let us come inside. They are superb people. I couldn't ask for better support. We got the first wheel off and it was so nasty, we needed to sandblast it and see how bad the others were."

Soon the cannon restoration "troops" realized that they were not going to be able to fix the wheels. But they refused to retreat. They decided to re-manufacture the wheels.

Enter young Jayson McGee, a welder, and Knightstown's Lloyd Hanson, a retired Chrysler Corporation millwright who had worked with Ingram at the plant. "Jayson and Lloyd got their torches out," Ingram said. "Then we started taking care of rusty parts on the cannon, knowing that more kids are going to climb on this thing. Then Randy's Sandblasting brought a mobile unit out and sandblasted the cannon on site."

"A very talented young man, Doug Dorn, was contacted and asked if he'd like to paint the cannon," Ingram continued. "We had some donors, Dennis Couch and Donnie McCorkle, who gave us some money to buy the paint." Once the cannon was ready to take back on the hill, Ingram and his team of restoration soldiers had another problem to solve. "That cannon was just sitting there," Ingram said. "It was not bolted down. It was not secure. It could have rolled down that hill."

Ingram proceeded to meet again with Robbins and purchase two half-inch pieces of stainless steel. Robbins set up one of the Magna machines to make pieces that replaced the worn-out rivets in the cannon. "Mitch Soliday and I went out, used Sakrete and filled depressions in. Then Jayson and I went out to bolt and seal those stainless steel pieces down. He welded two little stops that the cannon sits inside now. So it's not going anywhere."

The military restoration mission was accomplished with "tons" of volunteer help and zero tax dollars. Magna Machine and Tool provided the major monetary contribution to restore the cannon. "Without their support for resources and allowing Jayson to work on it during business hours, this would have taken much longer to complete," Ingram said.

"I can't say enough for the support we got from Magna, Jayson McGee, Lloyd Hanson, Randy and Scott Neal," Ingram added. "This was not a one-man show. I just got the ball rolling, and I got to stand in front of the microphone when it was dedicated, but no way could I have done this by myself."

Once restored, Hanson looked at Ingram, his longtime Chrysler friend, and said with a gleam in his eye, "Why don't we fire this thing?"

"Originally I said, no, no…." Ingram recalled. "We weren't really sure how to do it because the firing mechanism had been taken out." But after Hanson died on December 28, 2017, at the age of seventy-two, Ingram and McGee decided to figure out a way for the cannon to fire in tribute to Hanson and all military veterans. "We fired it three times at Magna Tool out in the boondocks to make sure it was safe," Ingram said.

Now the cannon is fired on special patriotic and military occasions. "We always pick out a military veteran, a Purple Heart or medal recipient to help us fire it," Ingram said.

Since completion of the restored cannon in 2018, the Walter P. Chrysler class of 1966 has been back for its traditional photo around the cannon. It makes Ingram smile. "I can't imagine anybody who lived in and around New Castle who hasn't seen that cannon," he said. "I took it as an honorable badge of duty to do this for our veterans of World War I and World War II. For that piece of equipment to be sitting at our Memorial Park and above our veterans museum in that condition was embarrassing to me."

Years from now, Addie and Kayson McGee, children of Jayson and Karis McGee, might well be climbing the restored cannon with their friends. "Hopefully someday they can say, 'Look at what my dad helped do,'" Ingram said. And that, no doubt, would make General Bundy smile.

PEARL HARBOR: DAY LIVES IN INFAMY FOR TWO HENRY COUNTY FAMILIES

For many years, Dawson Pope was a well-known carpenter in the Mooreland area. People appreciated both his skill and his wry sense of humor. What they may not have realized, however, is that this humble man was at Pearl Harbor on December 7, 1941—and that he used his talents to help rebuild the area decimated by the infamous Japanese attack.

"He was just a quiet, quiet guy about everything," one of Pope's sons, Curt, said in an interview with the *Courier-Times*. "I had deep respect for dad. I would typically try to call him each Dec. 7 and thank him for his service."

Sadly, Pope can't make that phone call to his dad anymore. Dawson Pope died on July 16, 2011, at the age of ninety-two. But he and his family—especially his mom, Lela, who was married to Dawson for sixty-four years—remember this day during a time when some fear people are paying less and less attention to it.

The statistics are sobering and the emotional pain behind the numbers indescribable:

- 2,388 Americans died in the attack
- 1,178 Americans were wounded
- 21 American ships were sunk or damaged
- 323 American aircraft were destroyed or damaged

It has been called one of those days in American history when people remember where they were and what they were doing when they heard the news. Lela Pope was only twelve years old when it happened. "We lived in New Castle at the time," she said. "Dad owned a home on E Avenue. I was sitting there on the floor, listening to the radio. I knew something was wrong."

What she didn't know then was the man she was destined to marry was there at the scene of all the chaos. Dawson Pope was twenty-two years old and on duty in the U.S. Navy. His son Curt remembers Pope telling him that he was stationed at the mouth of Pearl Harbor, away from the biggest part of the attack, yet way too close for comfort.

"He was stationed where the ships come into the harbor," Lela Pope said. "Of course, when they attacked, they came in over the airfield and crippled the planes before they bombed the boats. Then they flew over where Dawson was. Dawson said they were just getting out of breakfast when it happened."

"He told me Japanese airplanes were flying so low you could see the facial features of the pilots," Curt Pope said. "They had been on alert for a couple of weeks and just had come off of it when the attack happened. He could see the explosions."

"He made the remark to me once that if he'd had a rifle, he could have probably shot the pilot," Lela Pope added.

"They had secured all the ammunition in a complex and couldn't get into it in time to react," Curt Pope said. "He was sort of in a helpless situation."

Like many World War II veterans, Pope didn't talk much about his war experiences. "I don't know that anybody ever asked him a bunch of questions about it," Lela Pope said.

"Except me," Curt Pope said with a grin.

Pope said it took several proddings to pull information out of his dad. "I remember being about 6 or 7 years old and seeing a painted photo of Pearl Harbor in an encyclopedia book," he said. "It was the first time I realized this was a really big deal in the history of the United States and my dad was there."

Before Dawson Pope died, one of his grandsons interviewed him over the phone. Curt Pope and siblings Cheryl, John and Ross wanted to make sure that the family link to that fateful day was passed on to new generations. "I pulled out all my books related to Pearl Harbor and had dad sit down and talk about it with his grandsons. It seemed like every time you'd get him to talk about it, you'd find out a little bit more."

His military legacy lingers in the family. Curt retired from the U.S. Navy, was a naval flight officer and later helped with the Predator program for the U.S. Air Force.

While Dawson Pope was an innocent bystander in the attack, he became a hero of sorts afterward. His extensive background in construction helped the rebuilding effort. But then to Curt—who has visited Pearl Harbor several times over the course of his career—his dad was always a hero. "It's a gift to have someone larger than life to look up to," Curt said. "I remember looking up to people like Jacque Cousteau and Neil Armstrong before really understanding what my dad went through at Pearl Harbor and what he did afterward. I just have always had deep respect for dad."

While Dawson Pope lived to tell about Pearl Harbor, another Henry County man did not. His family didn't really learn of his fate until seventy-five years after the attack.

According to information from the Defense POW/MIA Accounting Agency, Navy Shopfitter Third Class Francis L. Hannon was assigned to the USS *Oklahoma*, which was moored at Ford Island, Pearl Harbor, when the Japanese attacked.

The USS *Oklahoma* sustained multiple torpedo hits, which caused it to quickly capsize. The attack on the ship resulted in the deaths of 429 crewmen, including Hannon. But Hannon's fate was unknown until many years after the attack. A letter dated December 16, 1941—just nine days after the attack—shared the family's sorrow about the event and overwhelming worry about the fate of their son. It was from Hannon's father:

Dear Father Will,

We are all grief stricken over hearing the terrible thing that happened at Pearl Harbor. Our youngest boy, Francis Leon, was aboard the U.S.S. Oklahoma and as yet we have no word from him, we thought perhaps you might be able to tell us where we could write to find out if he were among the list of casualties or if we would be able in times like these to find out if he were in a hospital there on the island. Do you know if all the names have been sent to relatives now?

It would not be until October 24, 2017, that Hannon's fate was confirmed. A Defense POW/MIA Accounting Agency press release announced that Hannon had been accounted for at last, with help from the U.S. Department of Veteran Affairs.

Hannon's name is recorded on the Walls of the Missing at an American Battle Monuments Commission site, along with the others who are missing from World War II. A rosette has been placed next to his name to indicate that he has been accounted for at last.

D-DAY: JUNE 6, 1944, MEN FROM HENRY COUNTY STORMED THE BEACHES, INCLUDING ONE WHO DIDN'T COME BACK

You are about to embark upon the great crusade toward which we have striven these many months. The eyes of the world are upon you....I have full confidence in your courage, devotion to duty and skill in battle.
—*General Dwight D. Eisenhower*

On June 6, 1944, Allied troops stormed the beaches at Normandy in what has been described as one of the greatest military invasions in American history. Gigantic newspaper headlines screamed the news: "Invasion Is Under Way. Allied Troops Land in France."

If December 7, 1941, is indeed a day that lives in infamy, then June 6, 1944, is one that provides constant echoes of heroism. A day so many died in order that others might live in freedom. A day that changed history.

This columnist's dad was there. Jim Radford—a Mooreland resident, town marshal and reserve deputy for the Henry County Sheriff's Department—was among those who stormed the beaches. He didn't talk a lot about those harrowing minutes from hitting the water to finding cover from enemy fire. I remember him telling us about removing pieces of equipment to stay afloat until he reached shore. Some of his fellow soldiers unfortunately drowned before they ever got to the beach due to the weight of their gear.

I also remember him talking about the bodies of fallen soldiers he had to navigate through and about the brave paratroopers coming down from the sky, offering just the slightest diversion that may have saved his life.

A newspaper from Henry County Historical Society files emphasized the impact of those paratroopers. "Berlin said that masses of Allied parachute troops bailed out over Normandy, trying to seize airfields. Just before taking off in the darkness, the paratroops were wished Godspeed by the lanky Kansas supreme commander, Gen. Eisenhower. He was accompanied by several other of his commanders and his face was tense but confident as he strode down the long lines of fighting men."

Above: Headlines in the June 6, 1944 issue of the *Courier-Times* alerted readers that the D-Day invasion was underway. *From the* Courier-Times.

Opposite: Jim Radford was among the troops at Normandy on D-Day. He lived to tell about it and served as town marshal of Mooreland for many years. *Cheryl May.*

On June 6, 1944, 160,000 Allied troops landed along a fifty-mile stretch of heavily fortified French coastline to fight Nazi Germany on the beaches of Normandy, France. Eisenhower called the operation a crusade in which "we will accept nothing less than full victory."

More than five thousand ships and thirteen thousand aircraft supported the D-Day invasion, and by day's end on June 6, the Allies had gained a foothold in Normandy. The D-Day cost was high—more than 9,000 Allied soldiers were killed or wounded—but more than 100,000 soldiers began the march across Europe to defeat Hitler.

Historians say that before the D-Day operation, Allied attacks against Germany and Italy had been in the south of Europe, far away from Hitler's homeland. D-Day represented the first real threat to Germany's control of western Europe. It opened up a second major front against Germany and convinced Russia to remain in the war.

Prior to D-Day, the Russians felt that they were the ones doing all the fighting against Germany in Eastern Europe. The invasion of Normandy was also a means of countering Russia's growing Communist influence in Europe. It was clear that Germany was going to be defeated at some future point. America and Britain were very concerned about what the Russians would do. The Russians might make a separate peace with Germany. This would leave Britain and America to fight on alone. Or Russia might successfully conquer Germany and control most of Europe.

D-Day stopped this from happening. The D-Day invasion—part of what was known as "Operation Overlord"—put Russia's fears to rest by opening a second front and eventually aided the Allies in stopping the spreading Communist threat in Europe.

If you haven't seen the movie *Saving Private Ryan*, it provides a horrifying glimpse into what the soldiers on Omaha and Utah beaches faced that day—and what they did.

A June 6, 1994 article in the *Courier-Times* on the fiftieth anniversary of the historic event also featured some other soldiers with local roots who were involved in D-Day. In addition to Radford, Sulphur Springs resident Francis Hale and Middletown resident Homer "Pedee" Peckinpaugh were among those who survived the invasion and lived to tell about the soldiers' push into Germany.

Sadly, Kennard native Richard Pitts Jr. apparently died during the invasion. His body was never found. In memory of Pitts's sacrifice, a marker was placed at McCray Cemetery in Wilkinson. The marker simply states that Pitts was reported missing in action on June 6, 1944. Pitts was among 105 local people who were killed during World War II. In all, more than 4,000 from Henry County served during that war.

World War II Veteran Back in the Cockpit at Age Ninety-Seven

Even at age ninety-two, the sky's the limit for those who dream. For World War II veteran Carl Crisp, a wish to fly in an airplane one more time was granted Sunday not by a genie, but through the caring hands of family, friends, local airport officials and the Senior Living at Forest Ridge staff in New Castle.

"He flew 35 missions over Germany in B-17s as a radio operator," Henry County Historical Society president Gene Ingram said. "Norma Kriner called me and said Carl had told her 'Boy, I wish I could go up in a plane one more time.'"

Soon, Ingram was on the phone to New Castle airport manager John Marlatt, who arranged all the details. When this past Sunday came, up, up and away Carl went. But it was so much more than an airplane ride.

There to greet Carl on the runway was his best flying buddy: youngest daughter Jana Anderson. The little girl who was a student at Wilbur Wright Elementary School in New Castle grew up reaching for the clouds. Inspired by her father, she wanted to earn her own wings. For many years, they both had pilot's licenses and flew together often.

"I grew up with aviation," Jana said. "We used to ride our bikes over to the Brown Road Airport and watch planes take off. My dad owned a plane and kept it hangared there. He was my mentor. I grew up in airplanes with him."

The 1978 New Castle Chrysler High School graduate was a cheerleader for the Trojans. She is now a nurse in the Dayton, Ohio area. But on Sunday, she was a cheerleader all over again—for her dad. "Daddy and I flew together to visit my grandma down in southern Kentucky," Jana remembered. "It was great daddy/daughter stuff. Great memories. Very special."

Henry County Historical Society board president Gene Ingram stands with World War II veteran Carl Crisp just before the ninety-seven-year-old flew an airplane one last time. *Gene Ingram.*

That made another surprise for Carl even more exhilarating. During the flight, the Marlatt Field pilot of the plane offered him the controls. Riding in the back seat of the plane with Ingram, Jana marveled at her dad's reaction. "Daddy took the yoke [steering wheel] of that airplane like he'd never forgotten," Jana said. "I watched the altitude and he just kept it so steady. It was amazing. It was just so touching to see my dad flying again. It was his dream to fly. He used his G.I. Bill to learn to fly."

"We flew for about an hour," Ingram said. "We flew over Delaware, Randolph and Henry counties." The man who worked many years at Indiana Bell/AT&T also received a special call during his flight. "The Henry County Amateur Radio Club was there to surprise Carl and even called him by his call letters—W9QPB," Ingram said.

When the plane landed, Carl and Jana were greeted by the Henry County Honor Guard, where the World War II vet was greeted with a solemn salute. "We had no idea the honor guard would be there," Jana said.

World War II veteran Carl Crisp was accompanied by his best flying buddy—daughter Jana Anderson. *Gene Ingram.*

World War II veteran Carl Crisp was surprised at the New Castle airport by an honor guard salute. *Gene Ingram.*

A fitting moment for an honorable man who was married to his wife, Rachel, for more than sixty-five years. A man who raised four daughters (Carla, a Delaware resident; Diane, who lives in Maryland; and Debbie, who lives in Richmond; along with Jana, a Dayton-area resident). A man who served his country honorably.

"It just all touches my heart," Jana said in summing up the experience. "I still love aviation, love every part of it. I live really close to the airport where I got my private pilot's license and my instrument rating. I flew lots of times during my training to visit my mom and dad. They would always meet me in New Castle or Anderson or Muncie. They were very, very supportive and cheered me on....So this was pretty special."

WORLD WAR II VETERAN CELEBRATES 100TH BIRTHDAY

Not many people live to be 100 years old. Even fewer, it would seem, can drive themselves to their own 100th birthday party. But that's exactly what Omrie Harmon did.

The World War II veteran named for a biblical king was indeed the man of the hour last Saturday at the New Castle VFW Hall. "Well, when you get to be 100, you ought to be a king," State Representative Tom Saunders told Harmon.

"I've been waiting 100 years to tell you this," local car dealer Lonnie DeHart teased Harmon as he wished his former business partner a happy birthday.

New Castle mayor Greg York said, "I don't know of a man that I'm any more proud of than Omrie Harmon."

As if the 100th birthday party wasn't impressive enough, family and friends had a second reason to celebrate: the 79th wedding anniversary of Harmon and his wife, Geraldine. They were married on February 14, 1942.

Fitting Celebration

Born March 20, 1921 to Elmer and Cloda Harmon, Omrie gave a look of astonishment when a reporter asked, "Can you still drive?"

"Well, heaven's yes!" he said. Omrie said he started driving when he was about fourteen or fifteen years old and "had a license before you had to have them."

World War II veteran Omrie Harmon greets well-wishers at his 100th birthday party. *From the* Courier-Times.

Omrie came dressed for the occasion. He was wearing his U.S. Army jacket, which still fit perfectly more than seven decades after he served. Omrie said that it was the first time he'd had the jacket on since being discharged in 1945. "It's not even tight," York said of Harmon's jacket.

While Harmon was the man of the hour, many in attendance said that the "honor" was theirs in knowing a man whose long life has been lived with such dedication and dignity. "What an honor it is to have somebody who has served our country, served our community and lived for the Lord," York said. "He started the Yellow Cab company, had a car lot for what seemed like a hundred years, knew how to run a business, figured life out, had a beautiful wife and family."

"Omrie, we are so grateful for you and your example, your legacy and your love for the Lord," York concluded.

War Stories

Gracious, funny and humble, Harmon made one thing perfectly clear during his 100th birthday celebration. "I am no hero," he said. "The heroes are the ones who passed away, who never made it back to the United States. And some of those were guys I knew in my outfit."

Harmon did have a unique military task during World War II. He drew maps for the D-Day invasion of Normandy to be used after the swarm of U.S. soldiers landed on the beaches. A mechanical draftsman, he said his top-secret assignment required armed guards outside his door while he and another soldier worked.

The big crowd of admirers erupted in laughter when Harmon told the story of his return to New Castle after World War II ended. "I caught a bus home," Harmon said. "I don't know if any of you remember how 14th and Broad used to be, but it was so busy at that time, you could hardly walk. I got off the bus and thought I saw my wife and his brother. They didn't know I would be coming home that day."

"Well, I thought I'd surprise my wife," Harmon continued. "I walked up behind her, grabbed her and gave her a big kiss— and saw that it wasn't even my wife. It was my wife's sister! You talk about being embarrassed."

This is how Omrie Harmon looked in uniform during World War II. He actually wore a military jacket to his 100th birthday celebration. It still fit. *Photo submitted.*

Omrie Harmon laughs after talking about "kissing the wrong woman" when returning from World War II duty. He hugged a woman from behind thinking it was his wife. After he kissed her, Harmon discovered it was actually his wife's sister. *From the* Courier-Times.

Presentations

There was no reason for Omrie to be embarrassed that day. Presentations in his honor were made by State Representative Saunders, York, Foursquare Church pastor Jim Becker and others. "He not only survived 100 years of life, the Great Depression and a world war, but also the virus," Saunders said in reference to COVID-19, which took so many elderly people early on.

In a normal year, Saunders said that Harmon would have been invited to the Indiana Statehouse and a resolution would have been passed in his honor, but that wasn't possible during the pandemic. "I have birthday greetings from the Indiana General Assembly," Saunders said. "I had an opportunity to meet with the governor on Friday. He wanted me to be sure and extend to you his best wishes and thanks for your service, not only for our country, but the State of Indiana. And he wishes you many more."

Judy King, a VFW chaplain and Iraq combat veteran herself, presented Harmon with colorful quilt. She said that he may be receiving something in the mail from U.S. Representative Greg Pence as well.

Eyewitness to Local History

Harmon was a living local history book at his 100th birthday party. He remembered when the Maxwell-Briscoe Automobile Factory was in operation. He talked about how his father-in-law would catch the interurban at Springport and ride back and forth to New Castle for his job at that factory. Then a reporter showed him a November 7, 1935 photo of a crash involving an interurban car and a fire truck in front of the New Castle Post Office.

"I remember when that happened," Omrie said.

Omrie said that he knew Sidney Baker, New Castle's first four-time mayor, for whom Baker Park is named. He remembered the infamous Perfect Circle strike here in 1955 and actually sent pictures of the scenes to the Associated Press. He talked about his dad working for the Hoosier Kitchen Cabinet Factory.

Speaking of dads, Omrie, who owned Harmon Motor Sales for thirty years, told Representative Saunders, "I sold your dad a car."

Looking Ahead

Talk of the Old Sears Building brought back memories for Omrie too. Not of shopping when Sears and Roebuck operated a three-story department store in downtown New Castle. Rather, of a roller skating rink on the third floor. "I think that's where I met my wife," he said.

When asked for the secret of their seventy-nine-year marriage, Geraldine simply said, "We believe the same way. We both love the Lord."

The one-hundred-year-old who still drives continues to have his eyes firmly affixed on the road ahead. "I was telling Tom I'm trying to catch my father," Harmon said. "He was 101."

Saunders summed up the grand occasion. "He tells me when he gets to be 102, he's going to slow down."

HENRY COUNTY MAN WAS DRIVING FORCE BEHIND DEVELOPMENT OF THE MILITARY JEEP

New Castle's manufacturing know-how put the city on the map in the first half of the twentieth century. It also helped win World War II.

Ward Canaday, a New Castle, Indiana native, was the mastermind behind creation of the military Jeep. *Doug Magers*.

Ward Canaday is the man who developed and built the Jeep, the sturdy automotive workhorse introduced for military use.

Born in New Castle on December 12, 1885, Ward was one of four sons born to Miles and Sara Helen Schmidt Canaday. He graduated from Harvard and began working for the Hoosier Manufacturing Company, innovators of the Hoosier Kitchen Cabinet. Eight years later, he joined the Willys Overland Motor Company in Toledo, Ohio.

It was there that Ward led creation of the General Purpose Vehicle or GP, pronounced "Jeep." Born in the heat of battle, the "Go Anywhere. Do Anything." Jeep Brand 4x4 emerged a hero to thousands of Allied soldiers around the world.

A man of vision, Ward "saw possibilities everywhere." He gave advice and an oft-used phrase was "Now I'll tell you what you ought to do…." Many in the military are glad the government listened.

Author Patrick R. Foster wrote a book dedicated to this transportation sensation. It's called *Jeep: The History of America's Greatest Vehicle*. "Few American vehicles, or vehicles made anywhere else in the world for that matter, are as universally iconic as the Jeep," Foster wrote. "From olive drab WWII military relics to the beloved Wrangler with its rear-mounted spare tire, open-air design, and telltale roll cage, the Jeep is a true classic."

Historians say that Jeep's early history is legendary. Its role in helping defeat the Axis powers during World War II is undeniable. On the battlefield, the Jeep was fast, nimble and tough. It could handle nearly any terrain, and when it did get stuck, it was light enough for soldiers to lift free. It towed anti-tank weapons that could be deployed quickly, and it could mount a machine gun for fighting infantry.

The Jeep also served as an ambulance on the battlefield. It forded rivers and traversed lakes, it came ashore on D-Day and it carried the Allies all the way to Berlin, onto Guadalcanal and Iwo Jima and, eventually, onto the mainland shores of a defeated Japan.

A restored Jeep is on loan to the Henry County Veterans Museum and on grand display in the museum. "The Jeep we have was manufactured by Ford using the Willys design," Museum board president Ed Hill said. "Willys could not meet the production demands, so the Army awarded a contract to Ford to also produce them. There were minor differences between the two, but the Army required that all parts be interchangeable. The owner of the Jeep told me that Henry Ford was so protective of his brand that every part put into the Ford built Jeeps had the Ford Script stamped on it, even the individual bolts had the Ford 'F' stamped on the head."

"There were nearly 650,000 Jeeps produced between 1941–1945 for the war effort," Hill concluded. "The museum's Jeep is complete and meticulously restored. It runs like new and has been seen in local parades over the years. It is configured for radio operation for the U.S. Army Signal Corp, and I was told the radio is fully functional."

And to think the idea came from someone born right here in Henry County.

Politics

Mooreland Man Comes "Within an Eyelash" of Being Indiana's Forty-First Governor

The year was 1960. New Castle Fieldhouse was just a year old. Sid Baker had just completed his record fourth term as mayor, with Walter Falck succeeding him. Nationally, the Space Race was just starting to heat up.

Meanwhile, in the small northeastern Henry County town of Mooreland, a favorite son who had risen to the ranks of lieutenant governor was seeking the highest political office in Indiana.

Crawford Parker, son of a veterinarian and second of ten children, a man who once worked as a butcher in a Mooreland grocery store, was involved in a political campaign that would become one of the closest in state history, taking him, as his own son Mac Parker described, "within an eyelash" of becoming Indiana's forty-first governor.

In a recent conversation with the *Courier-Times*, the younger Parker shared his memories of the 1960 governor's race through a behind-the-scenes, introspective eight-page paper he wrote about his dad's campaign.

Political Rise from Local Roots

A son of Herbert and Ethel Parker, the man who almost became governor, was born in September 1906. His father was away often, working in Chicago and taking the train home on weekends. But he was a strong family provider.

Crawford Parker, a public servant from the small Henry County town of Mooreland, came "within an eyelash" of becoming Indiana governor. Digital collection of the late Mike Bertram.

Almost all of Crawford Parker's brothers and sisters attended college. And college was what indirectly brought Crawford Parker to the little town of Mooreland.

It was at Central Normal College in Danville where he met and later married Angie Lucille Bouslog in 1926. They came to Mooreland because her father, Enoch Bouslog, owned a small general store there.

From there, it didn't take long for Parker to get involved in politics. He became a Republican precinct committeeman in the early 1930s and then Henry County clerk in 1942. In 1946, he was elected president of the Indiana County Clerk's Association.

The political rise was natural for Parker, according to his son. "There was no hint of any scandal and he was a very hard working and dedicated public servant," Mac Parker wrote of his dad. "He was very photogenic, had beautiful white hair, always a smile and was usually dressed in a dark suit that accentuated his hair."

In the midst of his second term as county clerk, statewide opportunity knocked. He was appointed assistant secretary of state and then to the Indiana Public Service Commission. The appointment was significant in that Parker, a Republican, was chosen for the role by Indiana governor Henry F. Schricker, a Democrat.

But Parker was accustomed to working through political differences. While his family had always been Republicans, his in-laws had always been strong Democrats. "My father and grandfather, Enoch, never discussed politics to my knowledge," Mac Parker wrote.

There would be much to talk about statewide in the years that followed, particularly after the man with Mooreland roots became lieutenant governor in 1956. Parker's record as secretary of state was, according to his son, characterized by a modernization of the corporation and securities departments and upgrading for all others. "Generally, he was recognized for running a very efficient office and providing outstanding service," Mac wrote.

But a minefield of unfortunate political circumstances, all out of his control, awaited the man who would come "within an eyelash" of being governor.

Slick Political Tricks by His Political Enemies Hurt Crawford Parker's Gubernatorial Campaign

Photogenic, congenial and personable beyond measure, Crawford Parker seemed destined for the governor's office. The Mooreland man knew how to cover all the bases. He was a common sight at county fairs and had his picture taken with almost every fair queen. He went to every Republican National Convention and had met Senator Robert Taft, President Dwight D. Eisenhower and Vice President Richard Nixon. His son, Mac, remembers him "as a better campaigner" than the man he hoped to succeed, Governor Harold Handley.

"He worked at remembering names and was never too busy to stop and talk to a voter," Mac Parker wrote of his father. "Because he knew all the county chairmen and precinct committeemen throughout the state, he was well-received almost wherever he went. By the same token, in the Statehouse, where he served as Assistant Secretary of State, on the Public Service Commission, Secretary of State and Lt. Governor, he knew almost all the secretaries and custodians and anyone else who worked there, and was never too busy to stop and talk. Many years later, when I went to the Statehouse and the State Office Building as an attorney, people who had known him years earlier still talked about how down to earth and what a great friend he was."

The younger Parker remembers at one particular state convention how his father knew many of the one-thousand-plus delegates on a first-name basis. "I can remember standing in line with him as the hundreds of delegates came through a reception line, and he was able to address almost each one by name," Mac Parker wrote. "He knew where they lived, had visited them at their home or place of business and knew about their family. I was amazed at his ability to recall this information."

So it was no surprise when Parker was the Republican Party's nominee in the 1960 gubernatorial race. It looked like the man with small-town roots was going to win big. But as his son eloquently wrote, a trio of circumstances beyond his control got in the way.

"During Handley's term as governor, two things happened which had a great effect upon the subsequent gubernatorial election," Mac Parker wrote. "During George Craig's previous term as governor, some criminal conduct had taken place in conjunction with highway right-of-way buying. Later during the Handley term, all these gentlemen were indicted, convicted and served time. This was used by Crawford's opponent, Matt Welsh,

This photo shows Crawford Parker being sworn into state office. He served both as Indiana secretary of state and lieutenant governor. *Digital collection of the late Mike Bertram.*

linking Craig, Handley and Parker because they were all in the Republican administration when this occurred."

Linking Parker, however, was dirty politics at its worst. "While my father was secretary of state, he and George Craig were not friends and had almost no contact," Mac wrote.

The second unfortunate circumstance, according to Mac Parker, was Governor Handley's decision to seek a vacant U.S. Senate seat in the middle of his gubernatorial term. But while running for the seat vacated by U.S. Senator Bill Jenner, Handley did not resign as governor.

"Had he done so, then Crawford as Lt. Governor would have become 'Acting Governor' and could have run later upon his own record rather than having to run as someone who had been in the same administration as Craig and Handley," Mac wrote. "These two events, the Craig Highway Scandals and Handley running for U.S. Senate in the middle of his term—neither of which involved Crawford directly—ended up having an important influence on the outcome of the 1960 gubernatorial race."

Even though Crawford Parker campaigned vigorously for him, Handley ended up losing to Evansville mayor Vance Hartke by 244,000 votes, just two years after being elected governor by a substantial margin. "The newspaper clippings indicate that this was the worst defeat of a State office holder since 1936," Mac Parker wrote.

Not surprisingly, Welsh used Handley's unpopularity against Crawford Parker in the 1960 gubernatorial race. "Welsh didn't talk about Parker or 'his opponent,' but he always talked about 'Handley-Parker,'" Mac wrote. "He used it so effectively that you thought 'Handley' was Crawford's first name."

The third circumstance impacting the 1960 gubernatorial election? Well, in a way, it involved an event in New Castle.

Perfect Circle Strike in 1955 Hurt Crawford Parker's Chances in 1960 Gubernatorial Election

Excitement was in the air when Henry County voters went to the polls in November 1960. The John F. Kennedy–Richard M. Nixon televised debates had added a new aura to the presidential campaign. Meanwhile, local voters saw a rarity on their ballots when it came time to vote for governor: a Henry County man, Crawford Parker, originally from the small town of Mooreland, was a serious contender for the highest political office in Indiana.

New Castle resident Jim Cole remembers the excitement that came with being a part of the Crawford Parker for Governor campaign. "It was my first real introduction to politics," said Cole, who later would run for mayor of New Castle. "Everybody loved Crawford. He was always well dressed and well spoken."

But Parker had forces working against him that day even his honest reputation and work ethic couldn't overcome, according to his son, Mac Parker. Part of it involved what happened in New Castle a few years earlier. Another dagger to his hopes came from the political machine that churned in the northernmost reaches of Indiana.

"During the Handley administration, there had been a long and bitter strike at the Perfect Circle Company in New Castle. Gov. Handley went to New Castle, got up on a police car and tried to, in effect, quiet what was almost a riot," Mac Parker remembered. "Later, shots were fired, the National Guard was called out and people were hurt. Unfortunately, this gave New Castle a very bad reputation as a Union town and made it very

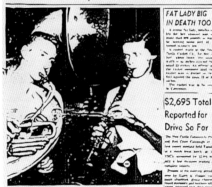

The *Courier-Times* headline on October 5, 1955, highlighted a sad time in New Castle industrial history, as a Perfect Circle factory strike turned violent. *From the* Courier-Times.

difficult for decades thereafter to get manufacturers to come to New Castle. Also, during the Handley campaign for senator, the right-to-work law was a big issue and Crawford made clear his stand that he was a supporter of the Right-to-Work law, supported largely by business groups and Republicans, to prohibit unions from mandating that non-members pay fees to the unions for representing them."

Ticket-Splitters Ruled the Day

Normally a deep red state, Parker remembers that "it had been hoped that Nixon running very strong in Indiana would carry the day" for his dad. But about 250,000 voters split their ticket on that fateful election day, and Crawford Parker ended up losing his gubernatorial bid "by an eyelash" according to his son. The final tally, percentage wise, was 50.39 percent for Welsh and 49.30 percent for Parker.

"Exit polls taken of voters at the time indicated that the highway scandals, Handley running in the middle of his term and the proposed repeal of the Right to Work, as I have indicated, were factors that caused voters to split their ticket," Mac Parker wrote. "Crawford finally lost by 23,000 votes. Nixon, on the other hand, carried the state by 250,000, so there had been a tremendous amount of ticket-splitting. To compound the loss, the Republican Lieutenant Governor, Richard Ristine, was elected. At that time, votes could split and did not have to vote for a Governor and Lt. Governor from one party."

The roller coaster of emotions and bitter pill of defeat were evident in Mac Parker's description of that night. "Pat and I worked transporting people to the polls in Fort Wayne all day, and then, after the polls closed, we left to go to Indianapolis for what we hoped was a victory celebration. At that point, Crawford was ahead and Nixon was running very strong in Indiana. The Lake County vote, which is always heavily Democratic, had already come in and Crawford was still ahead."

He continued, "However, from the time we left Fort Wayne until we got to Indianapolis, a second Lake County vote came in and the majority from Lake County was over 60,000, much greater than any previous Lake County votes."

Devastating Defeat, Suspicions of Fraud

It was a devastating defeat at the time. "The rest of the Republican State ticket was elected except for Phil Willkie as Superintendent of Public Instruction. Willkie, the son of Wendell Willkie, the Republican Presidential candidate in 1944 against FDR, was a maverick and the Indiana State Teachers' Association had campaigned very heavily against him. He lost by even more votes than Crawford did."

Mac Parker said that suspicions of vote fraud hovered after the election, particularly where Lake County was concerned. "A number of lawsuits were filed, but ultimately these were dismissed and the matter was turned over to the newly convened Indiana Legislature. The House of Representatives was overwhelmingly Democratic and the Senate was Republican. This resulted in a deadlock and nothing was ever done. Eventually, a significant amount of vote fraud was uncovered but the election was not disturbed.… The Democrat strategy of working television and radio—hitting hard on his connection to Handley and the highway scandals of George Craig and rallying the Union troops with the Right to Work repeal had been effective."

End of Political Ambitions, but Not Public Service

Crawford Parker never ran for office again after that election. But he also never forgot who he was and how important it was to serve.

While Crawford must have been bitterly disappointed, he never talked about it and, to a certain extent, never showed it. He completed his term as lieutenant governor. One of the final highlights was the dedication of the new State Office Building of which he had been chairman. "Because he was such a good friend, many people in the Statehouse took it much harder even than he did," Mac Parker wrote. "After his term was over, he took a position with Indiana Manufacturers Association as Administrative Vice President and continued for the next 10 years until his retirement. He took no more interest in politics, never supported a candidate or got involved in any way."

Unlike the election, Parker's achievements were not something any Democrat strategy could touch. As head of the Department of Commerce, Parker was instrumental in getting Indiana 3 between New Castle and Muncie dual-laned. And while the road to the governor's office was blocked for him personally, Parker would go on to make an appreciable difference for safer roads all across Indiana.

Mac added, "Later on, he received considerable publicity for an idea that he had turned over to the State Highway Department—that is painting a white stripe down each side of highways. This had not been done previously in Indiana or elsewhere and he came up with the idea while driving through the state campaigning."

SPORTS

AGNES RIFNER: "KICKING" DOWN BARRIERS LONG BEFORE TITLE IX

Devoted wife, mother and grandmother. Teacher. Homemaker. Oh, and one-time drop-kicker for her high school football team. Agnes Marie Rifner Schortgen was all of this. But what makes her life story especially unique is what she did one fall in 1943 as a New Castle High School student. Decades before Title IX opened the door for women athletes, Agnes Rifner was wearing a football uniform, trying to kick points after touchdowns for the Trojans. "Aggie," as she was affectionately known, died on February 10, 2019, in Fort Wayne at the age of ninety-one. But what a life she lived.

One Game, Instant Fame

Born in Mount Summit on June 5, 1927, to Oliver and Anna (Barth) Rifner, Aggie played in just one game. Yet that singular appearance in the Trojans' contest with Morton Memorial made her famous not only across the state but also nationwide and even, in a way, internationally.

"Back when she was playing, World War II was going on and she got letters from soldiers all over the world," said New Castle resident Stanley Rifner, a nephew of Aggie's. "A gentleman who had a radio program in Chicago or New York wanted her to come for an interview and offered to

Above: Stanley Rifner, a nephew of Aggie Rifner Shortgen, looks at the newspaper coverage his aunt received for being the kicker on the high school football team. *From the* Courier-Times.

Opposite: Ed Ogborne was an eloquent and passionate voice, both in newspapers and radio, during his journalism career. *Digital collection of the late Mike Bertram.*

pay all the expenses. But my grandparents, Oliver and Anna Rifner, said no. They felt like a lady just didn't do that back then."

To say that Aggie took a different path was an understatement. While her sisters were both destined to be nuns—one even serving as a teacher at St. Anne's Catholic School here in New Castle—athletics were always an important part of Aggie's life. She was intrigued by her elder brother, John, who was a fullback on Griz Baker's Trojan football team before graduating in 1939. He went on to fight in World War II, serving his country in North Africa. "They practiced where Eastwood school is now on 22nd

Street," Stanley Rifner remembered. "She started kicking the ball around in practice."

Courier-Times writer Ed Ogborne highlighted Aggie in one of his many poignant columns. "In the fall of 1943 she was a cute blond high school junior who used to wander over to the field where the high school team was practicing and casually drop-kicked nine out of ten tries through the

The Courier-Journal ROTO MAGAZINE OCTOBER 31, 1943

GRIDIRON GIRL
They won't let her play varsity so she kisses the boys goodby
Story and pictures inside 18-20

Aggie Rifner's one-game stint as the New Castle boys' varsity football team place kicker drew the attention of the *Louisville Courier-Journal*, which put her on the Sunday magazine cover. *Stanley Rifner.*

uprights, just for the fun of it," Ogborne wrote. "Aggie got so good at it, Coach Griz Baker figured there was no reason he shouldn't have a girl on his football team just to boot a few points after touchdown."

There was nothing in the Indiana High School Athletic Association rules against it—at least at first. But Stanley Rifner said that there was some family tension. "Dad didn't say much," Stanley said of Aggie's brother John. "I guess Uncle Bob really didn't like the idea."

Word spread like wildfire, even during a time with no social media, internet or twenty-four-hour television news cycles. "Agnes is our celebrity," the 1944 *Rosennial* stated. "Some schools have their Eleanor Holmes [a lawyer who broke several gender barriers], some have their Alice Marbles [women's tennis pioneer] but New Castle has its Agnes Rifner. Her picture has been featured in newspapers from coast to coast, because she is the only girl to have played on a high school football team."

Even the *Louisville Courier-Journal* featured Aggie in its Sunday newspaper magazine: "If you were out scouting for a football player, you'd look at pretty 16-year-old Agnes Rifner of New Castle, Ind. and then the scenery. After all, girls just don't play football."

"We Want Aggie"

Courier-Times archives captured the build-up of excitement about Aggie getting into a game. One story about the Muncie Central game that year said, "With a New Castle point after touchdown coming up, the crowd of 1,200 began to howl 'We want Aggie.'"

Aggie Rifner is seen here in an unlikely photo talking with boys' football teammates. *Stanley Rifner.*

Coach Baker disappointed the crowd on that night, but later that same month, Aggie got her chance. Although her two extra point attempts were unsuccessful, she had made history. "The ball game was highlighted by, perhaps for the first time in Indiana High School football, the appearance of a girl in a boy's grid game," the *Courier* reported.

IHSAA Intervenes

Among the many who took notice, however, were IHSAA officials. Soon, headlines of a much different nature were telling Aggie's stories, like "Girl Kicker's Case Up Before the IHSAA."

"It now seems as if Agnes Rifner, 16-year-old junior drop-kicker for the New Castle high school Trojan football team, has played in her 1st—and last—game," the article reported. "Principal J.R. Craw of the local high school said today he had received a copy of a special ruling made Saturday in Indianapolis by the Indiana High School Athletic Association's board of control forbidding participation in inter-school contests of mixed teams, including boys and girls."

The ruling was passed in a four-to-two vote. Interestingly, one of those dissenting happened to be A.L. Trester, the man for whom basketball's mental attitude award is named. Aggie took the ruling in stride, perhaps a key quality in a life she lived fully.

"Are you disappointed?" Coach Baker asked her.

"Yes, in a way," she replied.

"In what way?" Baker asked.

"Well, I just wanted to play," Aggie said.

Life After Football

As her life after high school unfolded, play Aggie did. She made Fort Wayne newspaper headlines more than once with her Senior Games efforts, where Aggie competed in table tennis, shot put, discus, horseshoes, swimming, biking, croquet and other track and field events.

Stanley Rifner remembers family gatherings in New Castle and Mount Summit, which naturally included some athletic competitions. "We'd meet at Memorial Park and sometimes at Lloyd and Daphne Williams' house in Mt. Summit," he remembered. "We'd play baseball in that big field he had south of the house." When asked if Aggie ever played, he replied, "Oh yeah."

A Rifner's name is on the New Castle Fieldhouse wall, but it's not Aggie's. Stanley said that Scott Rifner's name was there for his wrestling prowess. But he believes what his aunt did merits some type of recognition as well. "I really couldn't believe it until I started digging all the articles out," he said of his aunt. "It's like they opened a door to the past, because nobody in the family really talked about it."

Big Family Still Close

Aggie may not have kicked any extra points on the football field, but by all accounts, she was indeed a huge success in other aspects of life. She was mother to ten children, a family that's still so close, Stanley says they meet monthly and have a meal together.

Karann Hawks, a cousin to Stanley Rifner, recalled that Aggie and her husband, Bob, were toasted by national radio personality Casey Kasem, who dedicated a song to them on his syndicated countdown show. The song? "Through the Years" by Kenny Rogers.

They were married sixty-seven years, a union that ended when Bob died on February 3, 2019. Seven days later, Aggie followed. Her funeral was more of a celebration, however, in honor of a life well lived. A life lived fully and uniquely. A life that became a statement for girls everywhere, even as she was laid to rest. "Uncle Bob had male pall bearers," Stanley said. "She had all girls as pall bearers."

"The World's Largest and Finest High School Gymnasium"

When Chris May, executive director of the Indiana Basketball Hall of Fame, started planning a sixtieth-anniversary celebration for New Castle Fieldhouse, he made, in basketball terms, an outstanding pass to a man who was a sure shot to deliver.

The pass went to local basketball historian Neil Thornhill, whose presentation was nothing but net. Thornhill engaged and enthralled a crowd consisting of former players, coaches and fans in a trip down basketball's memory lane, providing a history of a facility that's not only served New Castle well but also put the entire community on a map of international proportions.

Thornhill called construction of the New Castle Fieldhouse "an idea that moved along in fits and starts over a 20-year period until the doors opened on Nov. 21, 1959." But he offered an interesting new twist on the old landmark's birth.

"To me, it really began March, 21, 1954," Thornhill said. "That night, Milan defeated Muncie Central to win the Indiana High School state championship in what most consider the biggest upset in state championship history. Their coach, Marvin Wood, becomes an instant statewide legend. Coincidentally, the New Castle coaching job becomes open."

In their efforts to lure Wood here, New Castle officials shared with him plans for building a new high school and gymnasium on the south side of town, Thornhill said. "The thoughts of not only moving to a bigger school that played in the premier basketball conference in the state [the North Central Conference] along with playing in a new basketball palace were very appealing," Thornhill said.

Well, the pitch worked. Wood became New Castle's head coach. But after two seasons and with the building of a new fieldhouse getting almost no traction, a frustrated Wood resigned at the end of the 1956 season with a year left on his contract, Thornhill said. "Had he known that a kid named Pavy, who turned out to be a pretty good player, was moving to town later that summer, he might have reconsidered leaving," Thornhill added, drawing laughter from the crowd.

The resignation of Wood and those unremarkable seasons became a blessing in disguise for those who have enjoyed watching games in the Fieldhouse for more than sixty years. "With the loss of a celebrated coach and several lackluster seasons, the New Castle-Henry Township Building Corp. was organized on Feb. 26, 1956," Thornhill said. "The sole purpose was to speed up the process of building a new fieldhouse."

More laughter came when Thornhill pointed out that the organization was formed less than a week after New Castle had lost to Knightstown in the sectional.

But Superintendent Rexford Wright said that the construction of a new high school had to take precedence. He indicated that a new physical education and basketball facility would have to be built at a later date.

New Castle basketball fans, tired of enduring games in the old "crackerbox" gym on Church Street, raised a rallying cry right then and there. Soon, the phrase "Gym Now" echoed throughout the town.

An advisory committee was formed. Ed Ogborne, a beloved local journalist with the *Courier-Times*, was elected president. Howard White, whose property south of New Castle would become "White Estates," became chairman of a fund drive.

A May 3, 1956 kickoff rally in Church Street gym started it all. And the community's "fast break" to raise $200,000 for building a fieldhouse was off and running. "This amount was raised without the benefit of any large donor," Thornhill said. "The largest was a corporate gift of $15,000. From there it went down to very small gifts from all sources in the community, not the least of which was a total contribution from the students themselves, who came up with nearly $4,000 raised from car washes, general work days and other fundraising projects."

Thornhill said on October 8, 1957, that the $200,000 goal was reached. In today's dollars, that's equivalent to $1.9 million. "The goal was reached in less than a year and a half," Thornhill said. Fast break, indeed.

With $875,000 from a bond issue and the $200,000 from the fund drive, construction began on December 30, 1957. Excitement was mingled with frustration on June 12, 1958, when steel work collapsed at the site, delaying the official opening by a year and preventing beloved local star Ray Pavy,

This is how the world's largest and finest high school gymnasium in New Castle started as a giant hole in the ground. *Doug Magers.*

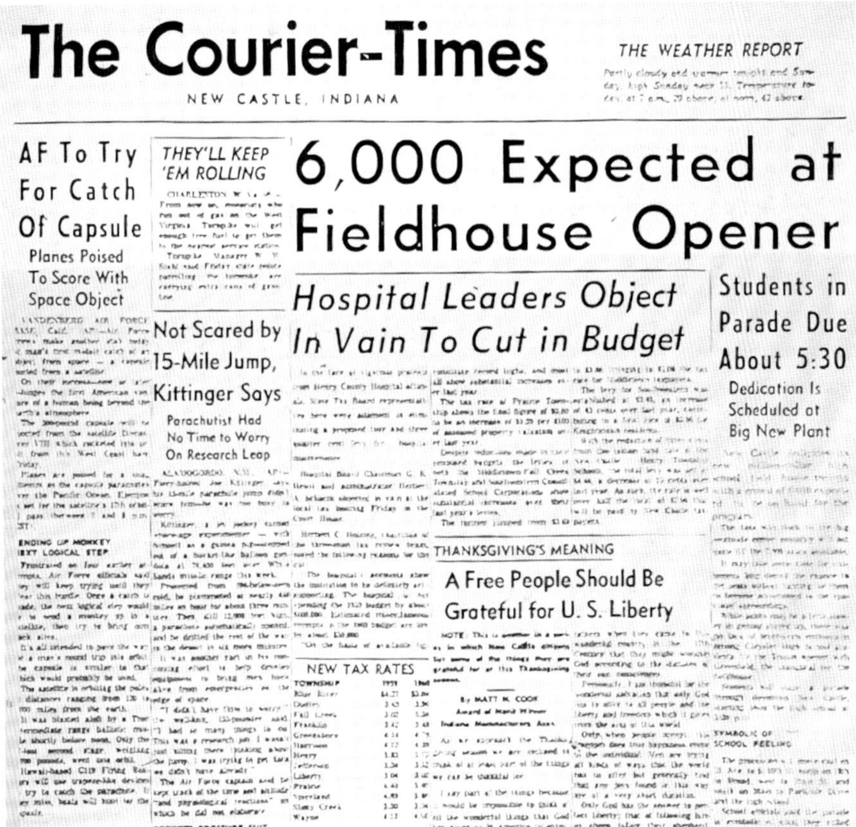

The Courier-Times

NEW CASTLE, INDIANA

THE WEATHER REPORT

6,000 Expected at Fieldhouse Opener

AF To Try For Catch Of Capsule

Planes Poised To Score With Space Object

ENDING UP MONKEY NEXT LOGICAL STEP

THEY'LL KEEP 'EM ROLLING

Not Scared by 15-Mile Jump, Kittinger Says

Parachutist Had No Time to Worry On Research Leap

REPORTS PRESSURE SUIT KEPT HIM COMFORTABLE

Hospital Leaders Object In Vain To Cut in Budget

NEW TAX RATES

Students in Parade Due About 5:30

Dedication Is Scheduled at Big New Plant

SYMBOLIC OF SCHOOL FEELING

TICKETS CONTINUE ON SALE LOCALLY

ANDERSON LETS GYM CONTRACTS

THANKSGIVING'S MEANING

A Free People Should Be Grateful for U. S. Liberty

By MATT M. COOK

First Aid Class Meeting Postponed To Mon., Nov. 30

Hearing Set Here On Union Charge Against Marsh

Rural Resident May Have Hip Fracture

Truck Bed Blaze Loss About $150

U. S., Russia Sign Pact

BASKETBALL SCORES

...hioan Killed in Crash North of Westport

The opening of the 9,325-seat New Castle Fieldhouse created exciting headlines. *From the* Courier-Times.

Construction of New Castle Fieldhouse hit a major snag on June 12, 1958, when part of the steel structure collapsed. *Doug Magers.*

who once scored 51 points at Church Street Gym, from playing in the facility during his senior year.

But fans were more than ready on the weekend of October 31–November 1 when an open house at the new Fieldhouse drew eight thousand people. Thornhill said that during that first year, two thousand season tickets were sold at $6.50 each for a ten-game season. "Many times over the years, New Castle's sold more season tickets than the Indiana Pacers," Thornhill said.

The official dedication game was played on November 21, 1959, as New Castle defeated Greenfield. In attendance was Indiana High School Athletic Association commissioner L.V. Phillips. It was he, not a New Castle official, who coined a most memorable phrase.

"In his opening dedication remarks on Nov. 21, 1959, IHSAA Commissioner L.V. Phillips stated he had been to a lot of high school gymnasiums in his role as commissioner, but this one has to be—and I quote—'the largest and finest high school fieldhouse in the world.'" Thornhill said. "An estimated 6,000 fans were in attendance that night, and the label has stuck."

Jerry Ellis: Letterman and Sharp-Shooter Supreme

Sixteen varsity letters in New Castle athletics. Eighteen awards for gallantry in 320 air force combat flights. One unforgettable life. On the court, in the field of play or over military conflict, Jerry Ellis was a hero in the hearts of many during his eighty-six years.

Ellis died on February 23, 2018, in San Jose, California, surrounded by family. In sports and military endeavors, he enveloped them and so many others with inspirational moments bound to live on for generations to come.

Ellis was born in 1932. It would be a poetic footnote to his life, considering that was the year New Castle's basketball team would win its first state championship; Ellis was destined to become one of the greatest Trojan athletes of all. "Jerry Ellis is the standard used to gauge all athletes since 1950," New Castle alum Jim Cole said.

His New Castle letter jacket on display at the Indiana Basketball Hall of Fame contained four emblems on the "N" representing the sports he played. Amazingly, he played each all four years of his high school career.

Bob Collins, a legendary sportswriter for the *Indianapolis Star*, said at Jerry's 2004 induction into the Indiana Basketball Hall of Fame, "Jerry was the only person he could find in Indiana to earn 16 varsity letters in basketball, football, track and baseball."

As a basketball player, Ellis helped New Castle win back-to-back regional crowns in 1949 and 1950. As a football player, he was named an All-American and later played three seasons for the Indiana Hoosiers.

Jerry Fennell, a columnist for the *Muncie Evening Press*, remembered one particularly exciting moment watching Ellis play on the gridiron. A son of Mr. and Mrs. Kermit (Mike) Ellis, the Trojan star shined especially for his father. "Jerry told his dad that the first time he carried the ball, he would score a touchdown for him," Fennell wrote. "After the kickoff, which he didn't return, he carried the ball from the Trojans' 19 and scampered 81 yards for a touchdown."

It was the first of twenty more touchdowns to come during the 1949 season. Ellis was captain of the football team both in 1948 and 1949. The 1948 Trojans went undefeated. The 1949 team lost just one game.

Ellis went on to Indiana University, where he played basketball and football his freshman year and then concentrated on football the last three years.

But while Trojan and IU Hoosier fans considered Ellis a sports legend, his true heroism was yet to come as a member of the U.S. Air Force. "He trained to be a pilot and flew almost every kind of plane," New Castle alum Herb

Jerry Ellis was perhaps the greatest all-around athlete in New Castle history, earning an unprecedented sixteen letters in four different sports. *From the* Courier-Times.

Bunch recalled. "When his four-year obligation was finished, he decided to make the Air Force a career and after 27 years, he retired as a colonel. His career took him all over the world, including Vietnam, where he earned the Silver Star and Purple Heart. He also had two tours of duty in Indonesia in the American Embassy, one as the top military officer."

In 1967, Fennell wrote this in the *Muncie Evening Press*: "Jerry really doesn't have much time these days to enjoy the fortunes of the Hoosiers.

Opposite: Former Indiana Basketball Hall of Fame director Chris May holds up the letter jacket worn by Jerry Ellis, showing the insignias of four different sports. *From the* Courier-Times.

Above: A close-up of the letter jacket worn by New Castle's Jerry Ellis shows its uniqueness—he competed in four different sports. *From the* Courier-Times.

He's Major Robert J. (Jerry) Ellis of the Air Force and is busy picking up more medals for his service in Vietnam than he did in high school, and that's doing quite a lot."

From September 24, 1966, until August 15, 1967, Ellis earned eighteen awards flying 320 missions. That included the Silver Star—the nation's third-highest combat award—for gallantry in connection with operations near Tuy Hòa, Vietnam, on April 10, 1967.

Fennell wrote, "Maj. Ellis took off at night from an unlighted airfield and directed air strikes by USAF fighter bombers and C-47 aircraft through hostile ground fire. Through his efforts, Maj. Ellis prevented the friendly position from being overrun and saved many lives."

While his life spanned great geographic distances, Ellis's New Castle roots run deep. Once a resident of P Avenue, he attended Parker Elementary School as well as junior high classes in the old Castle School across the street from the post office. He was a member of the First Presbyterian Church and sang in the youth choir.

A sentence in Ellis's obituary summed up not only his life but also the legacy he left behind: "Jerry was a phenomenal person, friend, father, uncle and hero. He will continue to be a hero in many of our minds and challenge us to be a better version of ourselves."

Iconic Phrase "March Madness" Originated in New Castle

Search Google on the World Wide Web for the phrase "March Madness" and you get more than 227 million hits. But the words now so closely associated with the NCAA men's basketball tournament can be traced to one source.

The year was 1931. The writer was Bob Stranahan, and he was sports editor of the *Courier-Times* in New Castle, Indiana.

Like the claim of having the world's largest and finest high school gymnasium, this one, too, can be verified. Chris May, former executive director of the Indiana Basketball Hall of Fame here in New Castle, brought the little-known fact to the attention of the *Courier-Times*.

"I'd heard that the phrase 'March Madness' had originated in Indiana referencing high school tournament time—and that's something we've continued to tell folks who visit our museum," May wrote in an email to *C-T* managing editor Travis Weik. "However, today [Wednesday, March 4] I found out something that I never knew."

May then referenced a recent column by Dr. Karissa Niehoff, executive director of the National Federation of State High School Associations (NFHS). Niehoff wrote that although the tagline "March Madness" became familiar to millions on a national scale in relation to the NCAA Division I Men's Basketball Championship, it was first used in connection with high school basketball.

"Scott Johnson, recently retired executive director of the Illinois High School Association…discovered through research that the first recorded mention of March Madness in relation to basketball occurred in 1931

March Madness

The elimination of Anderson, Tech, Columbus and Shelbyville were only mere flurries of what is to follow this week at the various basketball conventions in sixteen regional cities.

Candidates for the final election of the championship the following week-end in Indianapolis will be nominated in these conventions with 64 nominees seeking office at this time. Three-fourths of them will be eliminated this week • • • and the big problem for the people who pick is just which sixteen is to survive the first rush.

At Anderson it should be Alexandria. "Rube" Orner's ball club was good enough to upset the Indians, so they should be tough enough to eliminate Tipton and the winner of the Shortridge-Danville game. Either Kendallville or Auburn should come out of the Auburn regional. Shades of Tack Prentice! They must still play basketball at Kendallville!

At Bedford the Mitchell cagers should be able to weather the storm. Mitchell came through the sectional with flying colors and her regional competition is not exceptionally stiff.

Here is the first recorded use of the phrase "March Madness." National high school officials say it's the earliest use of the phrase they could find, dating back to 1931. *From the* Courier-Times.

by Bob Stranahan, sports editor of the New Castle *Courier-Times* in Indiana," according to the National Federation of State High School Associations article "The NFHS Voice: March Brings State Basketball Tournaments and Talk About the Shot Clock."

So, this writer took a short trip to the New Castle–Henry County Public Library for a deep time-travel look at the *Courier-Times* archives. And there it was—on the left-hand side of the Tuesday, March 10, 1931 edition. Under the column heading "Markin' 'em Up" was a headline that simply said "March Madness."

Bob Stranahan was a native of Matthews in southern Grant County but later moved to New Castle and graduated from high school here. He worked at the *Courier-Times* beginning in 1926 and "attained a wide reputation as a high school basketball writer." So wide, in fact, that he later became sports editor at Richmond and went to do the same job for the *Indianapolis Star* in 1937.

Stranahan's other credentials included membership in the Indiana Sportwriters and Broadcasters Association, National Baseball Writers Association and the Indiana Press Club.

After reading some of Stranahan's columns, one gets the impression immediately that he was quite capable of coining an iconic phrase. Here's a sample: "Just one more day of rest, and then all the whooping and hollering in the county will be turned loose. Goodwin gym will be a nice quiet place for a gentleman with an earache to spend the weekend—in misery."

Stranahan had a good-natured give-and-take for years with the *Muncie Star*'s Bob Barnet:

Robert Aloyius Barnet writes things for the Muncie Star, and Robert Aloyius is very amusing…today he has quite a lengthy piece about Charles "Micky" Davison. Mr. Barnet is quite vexed at Mr. Davison, who forwards and guards on Pete Jolly's basketball club…oh quite vexed. It seems that Micky has contracted pink-eye…only to have Mr. Barnet wind up saying "it will take more than the pink-eye to stop their Mr. Davison." Perhaps if the pink-eye won't stop Mr. Davison, maybe New Castle's Bob White can accomplish the feat!

After New Castle lost a tight regional game to Muncie Central that year, failing to protect a late lead, Stranahan was philosophical, if not poetic: "Speaking of that four-point lead…'tis better to have led and lost than not to have led at all."

Of course, New Castle basketball aficionados know what happened the year after 1931. "March Madness" had an exhilarating ending in 1932, with the Trojans winning the state championship.

Stranahan, who died on November 15, 1965, was married to New Castle resident Florence E. Duva. He is buried at Lincoln Memory Gardens Mausoleum in Whitestown, just outside Indianapolis. But oh, how his phrase lives.

REMEMBERING THE PAVY-RAYL SHOOTOUT

Sixty-five years have come and gone, yet there are people who still remember what happened at Church Street Gym on February 20, 1959, like it was yesterday. "What a fantastic game to see!" David Laird said on the Henry County Historical Society Facebook page. "The Cracker Box was bursting at the seams, maximum capacity! A game I will never forget."

That night, as many as two thousand people were crammed into the 1,800-seat gym attached to the YMCA as New Castle and Kokomo battled for a North Central Conference basketball championship. Janet Dyer, a classmate of Ray's, was there along with Jill Lough Chambers. Sally Selke Hale was also there, sitting on the Church Street Gym stage.

It is a game that refuses to fade from Hoosier basketball lore. Two Facebook posts by the Henry County Historical Society garnered a combined total of fifteen thousand "people reached."

When it was over, New Castle had prevailed, 92–81, but overshadowing the result was the official scorebook, which showed that Ray Pavy had scored an unbelievable 51 points, while Jimmy Rayl, his Kokomo counterpart, had finished with 49.

A decorative basketball commemorates the Ray Pavy–Jimmy Rayl shootout, one of the most memorable games ever in Indiana basketball lore. *Chad Niccum.*

The game captured both the attention and angst of legendary Indianapolis sportswriter Bob Collins. "Two of the greatest shooters of our generation or any generation, for that matter, met head-on at New Castle Friday," Collins wrote. New Castle won it, 92–81, but the game was lost in the sheer beauty of watching two tremendous shooters practicing their trade as no two boys ever did in one game. New Castle's Ray Pavy scored 51 points, Kokomo's Jimmy Rayl scored 49…and Collins was not there, a fact he won't brood over for more than the next 10 to 15 years."

It was a battle between two of Indiana's best teams, as the tenth-ranked Trojans took on the fourth-ranked Wildkats.

Pavy got off to a slow start, scoring only two field goals in the first quarter. But he had twenty-one in the second quarter and finished the game hitting twenty-three of thirty-eight shots from the floor to go with five for eight from the free throw line.

Pavy's 51 points set a Church Street Gym record and a one-game NCC mark, breaking the 48-point effort set by none other than Jimmy Rayl.

While Pavy scored many of his points on relentless drives to the basket, Rayl threatened to set the Church Street Gym rafters on fire, hitting ten of his first fourteen shots. He had 27 points at halftime. Rayl finished eighteen of thirty-three from the floor and thirteen of fifteen from the free throw line.

On January 16, 2009, Pavy and Rayl sat down to discuss it all again on the fiftieth anniversary of the Church Street Shootout. "Jim and I were

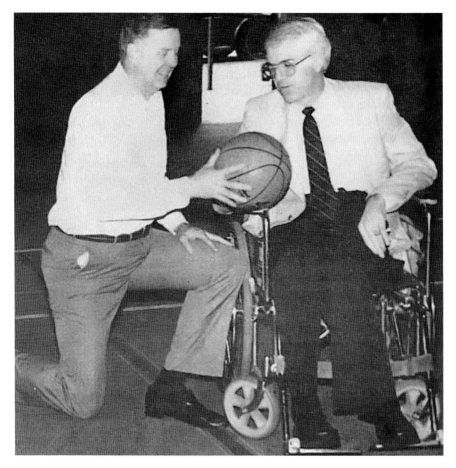

Jimmy Rayl (*left*) meets with Ray Pavy at Church Street Gym in October 1986 to discuss their famous shootout of February 20, 1959. *From the* Henry County News Republican.

playing for teams that were playing for the conference championship, and you've got to remember pro basketball for all practical purposes didn't exist in Indiana," Pavy explained. "It was not a banner year in college basketball. It was a golden era. We had tremendous coverage by the state newspapers and they sort of liked Jim and I, I think. We were fortunate not only to play on good teams, but we got good coverage, too. And we were winning, too."

Rayl was an explosive scoring machine at the time. "Leading up to that game, we were playing Muncie Central which was ranked number one in the state and undefeated," Rayl remembered. "And we beat them 72–70."

Left: Dr. Ray Pavy was a New Castle Community School Corporation administrator and community advocate for many years. *From the* Courier-Times.

Right: This New Castle yearbook photo shows Ray Pavy eyeing a free throw. *From the* New Castle Rosennial *yearbook*.

While they combined for 100 of the 173 points in the game, each could have scored even more. Incredibly, Pavy remembered missing "five wide-open layups" during the game. Meanwhile, if Rayl had the luxury of the 3-point shot, there's no telling how many he would have had. "Rayl hit shots from the center circle, and Pavy was relentless!" Laird said in a Facebook post.

Another popular Indianapolis sportswriter, Bob Williams, included the famed game in his 1982 book *Hoosier Hysteria*. He included comments from Pavy about what was going on inside the Trojan huddle to load "the shootout" with a winning strategy.

"We started running a forward split and Bill Fisher said 'I think I can go up and sit in the crowd and Thurston [Kokomo's Roger Thurston] will come right up and sit along with me," Pavy was quoted as saying.

"By gosh, let's try that," Coach Randy Lawson reportedly said.

"Fisher would come down, fake inside and then oftentimes stand clear out of bounds…and sure enough, Thurston would stand there right alongside," Pavy told Williams. "So I'd just take it right down the lane. It wasn't a matter of great genius on our part. We just took what was open and used it as long as we could get it. I got all the inside stuff and Jimmy bombed the eyes out of the basket outside."

Pavy called Rayl one of the best outside shooters he'd ever seen. "He was a great outside shooter," Pavy said. "In fact, that was the best range I ever saw except maybe against Minnesota in college. We were at Indiana together, and he had great range that night, too—scored 56 points against Minnesota, set a Big Ten record, and I believe we lost the game."

New Castle won on this night thanks in large part to a player other than Pavy. "The difference in the game for New Castle was John Lee's 20 points," Stephen Himes said of the late 1960 graduate.

Sadly, both men are gone now. Rayl died on January 20, 2019, at the age of seventy-seven. Pavy died on May 16, 2022, at the age of eighty.

Today, Church Street Gym is still in use as a community center. Just two years ago, it served as a site for COVID-19 vaccine shots for the public. But those other shots of yesteryear—the ones taken by Ray Pavy and Jimmy Rayl—will, as Collins once wrote, "be described as long as Hoosiers maintain their reckless romance with basketball."

Remembering the "Other" Shootout

Any Henry County basketball fan serious about "Hoosier Hysteria" history knows of the Ray Pavy–Jimmy Rayl shootout at Church Street Gym, the night Pavy scored 51 points and Rayl finished with 49. That date, February 20, 1959, has and will continue to live in basketball lore. Far fewer, perhaps, know that about a year later, another Henry County sharpshooter was involved in a similar shootout.

The date was February 12, 1960. Knightstown's Sam Chase led his Panthers into a battle at Batesville. Chase lit up the scoreboard for 47 points that night, while the Bulldogs' Ben Wernke finished with 45, as the Panthers topped the Bulldogs 93–73.

Chase said that it was probably a very similar atmosphere to the Church Street Shootout. "It was one of those games when there was more than standing room–only," Chase said.

Knightstown's Sam Chase starred from 1956 to 1960.
Indiana Basketball Hall of Fame.

Unlike the New Castle–Kokomo game, however, it was not on the radar of many fans. While the major Indiana newspapers covered the North Central Conference in detail, sportswriters at bigger newspapers then paid little attention to smaller schools like Knightstown and Batesville.

"Our team didn't get much notoriety outside of Henry County," Chase remembered. "The New Castle paper would maybe pick up something now and then. But elsewhere, there was no way for anybody to know you were doing anything but baling hay."

Chase laughs when he thinks about that night and scenes from the hit movie *Hoosiers*, parts of which would be filmed more than two decades later on the same Panther court he starred on from 1956 to 1960. Chase finished his career with 1,178 points, thirty-first-best in Henry County history. "To go on a road game in those days, it was just like in the movie," Chase said. "You'd have a caravan of cars behind the team bus. Batesville back then was considered a long drive. I don't know how it ever got on the schedule." Batesville is a fifty-one-mile drive from Knightstown.

Chase said the game was "rough and tough," with fans almost on top of the players from bleachers that were right up against the basketball court baseline. More difficult than the rowdy fans, however, was the Batesville defense. Like Pavy, Chase was public enemy number one on any opponent's chalkboard. "They were running a box-and-1 that I'd faced a lot, as did Ray and Jimmy," Chase remembered. "That night, they played the box real tight inside to keep me from driving, so I had a lot of outside shots."

Wernke was an impressive multi-sport athlete who once scored six touchdowns in a football game, finished second in the mile run at the state track meet and earned a tryout with the Cincinnati Reds as a pitcher and first baseman.

Wernke said he didn't remember much about that night, but his younger brother, Michael, does. He was there too. "He was a six-foot Oscar Robertson," Michael said of his brother. "He could out-rebound anybody that was 6-6."

Meanwhile, Chase was one of the hottest shooters in Indiana that year. Just a week before the Batesville game, he tied Knightstown's all-

SAM CHASE

ALL TIME LEADING SCORER AT THE HOOSIER GYM.

41 POINT RECORD

time single-game scoring mark with 41 points in a home game against Charlottesville. It remains as the most points ever scored by an individual in historic Hoosier Gym.

At Batesville, he hit sixteen of twenty-six shots from the floor and fifteen from nineteen from the foul line. His 47 points was a Knightstown school record that lasted for thirty-four years before Aaron Brown broke it with a 49-point effort in 1994.

Opposite: Historic Hoosier Gym, where the hit movie *Hoosiers* was filmed, pays tribute to Sam Chase with this poster. *Hoosier Gym*.

Left: Knightstown's Sam Chase (42) was one of the state's hottest shooters during the 1959–60 season. *Hoosier Gym*.

Chase fought through more than just double-teams and zone defenses targeting him. "I was having bad ankle problems," Chase remembered. "My feet were in tubs of water often. I had shots before games and had to get ankles taped to keep the swelling down."

Another memorable game found Chase's teammates in "hot water" that had nothing to do with ankle therapy. It was the night before a big game with neighboring Charlottesville. Chase was the last one to leave practice, again because of his ankle getting taped. "The doc and I walked out together," Chase remembered. "I went home and the next morning I get called into the principal's office."

School officials had decided to fill a Coke machine the night before in preparation for the game. What they didn't count on were players helping themselves to a drink on their way home from practice—without permission. "It infuriated the whole community," Chase remembered. "Right and wrong was big in the 1950s. The school officials were telling

Sam Chase. *Hoosier Gym.*

me I was going to be the only player aside from jayvee players on the court that night against Charlottesville. The rest of the team was suspended for that game."

It turned out to be a blessing in disguise for Chase. "That was the only time my younger brother, Pat, and I ever played together," Chase said.

And what a game it was. Sam Chase finished with 41 points, while his brother, Pat, snared 14 rebounds. In spite of having just one varsity player on the floor, Knightstown won big, 70–53. John Pidgeon, the longtime president of Draper in Spiceland, was one of the other sub-varsity players in that game and had an impressive 15-point, fourteen-rebound performance.

"We were all freshmen and sophomores, and Sam was the only senior," Pat Chase remembered. "Tom Mayhill [longtime *Knightstown Banner* publisher and member of the Indiana Journalism Hall of Fame] told me several times that the Charlottesville game was one of his most favorites."

UNFORGETTABLE EVENTS

DEDICATED NEWSPAPER REPORTER WALKS TO WORK
THROUGH BLIZZARD OF '78

It was Thursday, January 26, 1978. When a thirty-six-hour storm known now as the infamous "Blizzard of '78" hit, two dedicated *Courier-Times* staff members took on a postman's attitude. Neither snow nor ice nor wind would keep them from reaching the newspaper office and helping publish another daily edition. Their dedication became news, even though there was no newspaper issue to report it.

Betty O'Neal Giboney, a revered reporter here who worked here for forty-five years and lived to be one hundred, wrote about her experience of walking more than two miles to work that day, only to find the newspaper office closed.

"I had been reared in the show-must-go-on tradition," wrote Giboney, who in her younger years had performed as a New York City Roxyette dancer, forerunners to the Radio City Rockettes. "Anyway, if the *Courier-Times* was to put out a blizzard edition, I intended to be a part of it."

A world traveler, Giboney wrote that she had been to Antarctica a year earlier. "It had taught me how the well-dressed adventurer gets herself together," Giboney wrote. "So in preparation, I had put on—in addition to my usual winter dress—woolen slacks, over which I stepped into water-repellant, wind-resistant slacks and then had put on my waterproof, insulated cleated boots."

"That done," she continued, "I slipped into a woolen Norwegian ski sweater and over that my beaver coat. On my head, I wrapped two woolen hoods, one over the other, and swathed my face in a woolen scarf. To protect my hands, I put on one pair of woolen gloves and another pair of insulated mittens."

"I stayed comfy and warm for the whole trip," Giboney added.

When she finally arrived at the newspaper office, however, Giboney found no one else was there except advertising representative George Bonham. "Betty Giboney and George Bonham, unbelievably, came to work Thursday morning," a *Courier-Times* article reported. "Both found the door lock frozen shut, and both found it hard to accept that no one inside was working."

Betty Giboney once famously walked more than two miles through the "Blizzard of '78" so she could get to work at the *Courier-Times*, only to find the doors locked. The storm marked the first time in the newspaper's long history that it didn't print. *From the* Courier-Times.

During the Blizzard of '78, the newspaper did not publish either Thursday, January 26 or Friday, January 27 of that year. "It's not news now—just a bit of sorry history," a January 28, 1978 article read. It was believed to be the first time in the newspaper's long, long tenure that issues did not roll off the presses.

Mayor Greg York remembered just how bad it was. "Forty-three years ago today, I walked across State Road 103 at Riley Road and the snow drift was so tall, I was eyeball-to-eyeball with the stoplight and could literally touch it walking to Marsh's Supermarket," York said. "That's how deep the snow drift was."

Unexpected Snowstorm Turns Basketball Sectional into Slumber Party

There's a time-honored belief that basketball tournaments bring out the worst in Old Man Winter, who apparently isn't a fan of the game. Perhaps the origins of this belief began on February 25, 1961. On that particular Saturday, a surprising 8.5-inch snowfall came blowing into New Castle while the sectional semifinals were being played at the Fieldhouse.

Suddenly, the world's largest and finest high school gymnasium became the biggest slumber party in the city's history. "Hundreds of cars dotted the Fieldhouse parking lot this morning to provide an almost comical reminder of the blinding blizzard which trapped several thousand basketball fans in the huge arena Saturday," the February 27, 1961 edition of the *Courier-Times* reported.

According to the newspaper report, snow started shortly before the first game of the sectional tourney at 12:30 p.m. that Saturday. "By the time the second game had ended about 4 p.m., the blizzard had reached its peak," the newspaper reported.

David Burns remembered that night well. He and his girlfriend, Celia, tried to leave the building, but as fate would have it, his vehicle was white. Trying to find a white car in a snowstorm proved to be an impossible task. Not many others were having luck either. "Many fans tried in vain to find their autos," the newspaper reported. "Others found their cars but were unable to move them. Some pulled from their parking spaces into exit paths and were bogged down, tying up all traffic in the vicinity."

A nine-year-old Neil Thornhill remembers how he and his parents tried in vain to find their vehicle. "The snow was so bad, we couldn't find our car," he remembered. "My mom, dad and I walked all the way down to the motel and spent the night."

While the Fieldhouse had the biggest slumber party, other houses in town also hosted miniature ones because of the weather. "I was living on 18th Street," Mike Bergin said. "The National Guard brought some people in a truck and they stayed all night at mom and dad's house."

The *Courier-Times* reported that an estimated three thousand to four thousand "anxious persons" remained in the large arena at 6:00 p.m. "Small groups gathered in the sparsely populated stands. Hundreds of others wandered aimlessly around the rim of the structure—some hungry, some tired, all of them undecided," the newspaper said.

But as the night wore on, the moods of many lightened. In some cases, it was almost like a party. "Youngsters were sailing lids from paper drinking cups out onto the empty playing floor," the newspaper reported.

Gene Ingram was a seventh-grade student at the time. "It was a blast for us," he remembered. "This was a way we could stay out late and not have to go home. Decks of cards were at a premium."

"It turned out to be quite a party at the fieldhouse," retired New Castle educator Evelyn Rentchler said. "Even though it was miserable outside, people were fed, dry and relatively comfortable."

Jack Renner was in charge of concessions that day. "We had quite a few supplies but ran out about midnight," he said. "People were really very considerate about everything. Once they realized they were going to be there for a while, they relaxed and had a good time."

Eaton's Market—located just down the road from the Fieldhouse in the vicinity where Mancino's is today—delivered cold meat, jelly and bread for sandwiches, pie and doughnuts. Later Ray's Drive-In set up another concession stand in the corner of the building.

It was one of those moments where patience and kindness rose above the drifting snow—both inside the Fieldhouse and out on the snowy streets. "Some kind soul stopped and piled as many people in his vehicle as possible, taking them to a home," Rentchler said.

"I think that was typical of New Castle then—as it is today," Renner said. "This community has always been one to reach out and help others in need."

But there is a time-honored belief that whenever "Hoosier Hysteria" or March Madness or whatever you call these wonderful basketball tournaments are held, a grumpy Old Man Winter is lurking, perhaps jealous that he could never play the great game. "Since then, I think people have been a little leery of sectional tournament weather," Jim Cole said.

New Castle Residents Among Victims of Indianapolis Coliseum Explosion

H. Ray Edwards, a well-known New Castle jeweler, decided that he didn't like his seat during a Holiday on Ice performance at the Indiana State Fairgrounds Coliseum. So he and his wife decided to leave a local party and move to a better location. That decision on October 31, 1963, may have saved his life.

A gas explosion rocked the facility a short time later, killing seventy-four people and injuring nearly four hundred. Among the victims was a rural New Castle man, sixty-year-old Josiah Hutchens, and Mrs. Nellie Sherman Marshall, who had been visiting the area. Hutchens, a farmer, was a two-term member of the Henry County Council.

Retired local jeweler and community leader Morris Edwards remembered his dad talking about that night. "He talked about how lucky they were to have moved over," Edwards said. "I didn't know anything about it until I heard him telling the story the next day."

The two New Castle victims were among fifty-four people killed at the scene. Another twenty later died of injuries. At least eighteen families lost more than one member.

The Friday, November 1, 1963 edition of the *Courier-Times* included a first-person account of the disaster from another member of the group, Helen Rinsch. She was seated directly across from the section where the tragedy occurred. "It was horrible, after the terrible bang and the bodies were blown onto the floor, there was a tremendous flame that I thought would cause more damage than it did. Then debris began to fall and it mashed a lot of people."

"I don't know how anyone in that particular section came out of it alive," Rinsch added. "The bleachers blew out like they were made of cardboard."

Associated Press reports at the time said that many victims were charred by flames or crushed under tumbling structural concrete slabs. The show was minutes away from ending when the tragedy occurred.

"It was a full minute before people realized that it was real," Rinsch said. "Then people had sense enough to get up and walk out of the coliseum. Many of the people were covered with blood. People were cut by the cement."

The *Indianapolis Star* reported that propane gas had leaked from a rusty tank in a concession area, slowly filling the unventilated room. When the gas came in contact with an electric popcorn machine, a blast of orange flame reportedly shot forty feet up through the south side seats, throwing people and chairs into the air.

New Castle resident Arthur Peterson told the *Courier-Times* then that he had seen "nothing like it since World War II." "People were buried under chunks of concrete weighing 300 and 400 pounds," Peterson said. He volunteered to drive his station wagon as an ambulance all night to help victims.

More than just H. Ray Edwards were counting their blessings. Mr. and Mrs. Earl Stoops were seated just above the disaster but received only minor injuries.

While it was, as the *Indianapolis Star* put it, "the most deadly disaster in Indianapolis history," New Castle resident Floyd Fields saw many inspirational sights that he shared in a later *Courier-Times* article:

> *I saw men bleeding profusely from head wounds helping to lift large blocks of cement to free a total stranger.*
>
> *While struggling desperately, along with Art Peterson, to free my wife, up came two strangers and gave us the extra lift we needed to raise the slab of cement and lift her over another slab propped at a crazy angle. We were*

only about 20 feet from the raging inferno blazing 30 feet in the air. None of us knew but what another explosion might erupt any second.

At Community Hospital, I saw five nurses who had been on private cases all day come in one taxi to volunteer their services. At Methodist Hospital, several college students and young people were begging for an opportunity to give blood.

These things I saw. No doubt they were duplicated in every hospital in Indianapolis.

People can be wonderful.

MEMORIES OF JFK ASSASSINATION LIVE ON SIXTY YEARS AFTER THAT SHOCKING DAY IN DALLAS

No cellphones beeped or buzzed. The words *text* and *alerts* were never used together. Web sites were still the exclusive property of spiders.

But news of President John F. Kennedy's tragic death on November 22, 1963, still traveled fast. The shock waves turned normally noisy places like school hallways and department stores into library-like somberness and silence. From the sudden silence at a local grocery store to the sound of "Taps" on a CB radio, the events in Dallas on November 22, 1963, created a lasting impact on Henry County citizens.

Two local teaching veterans offered reflections on where and how they heard the news. Richard Ratcliff, county historian and longtime New Castle educator, was teaching a history class when the school principal paid an unexpected visit to the class. "I was in front of my eighth grade history class," Ratcliff said. "My principal came in and said he heard on the radio that the president had been shot in Dallas. It wasn't long before he returned with the news that the president was dead. This was long before each classroom was equipped with a television."

Rural New Castle resident Dave Hamilton was also teaching that day. "I was in my second year of teaching at School No. 75 in Indianapolis," Hamilton remembered. "Our school did not have a public address system and the principal delivered the sad news personally. It changed the tone of even junior high and elementary students for the rest of the day....When Carol and I stopped at a department store on the way home, it was extremely quiet for such a place. It felt like being in a mortuary."

Interestingly, two local residents had met Kennedy before that fateful day. In fact, one—Morris Evans, who was Veterans Services Officer here and also ran for mayor of New Castle—actually shook hands with Kennedy that morning as he and his wife, Jackie, greeted people after arriving in Dallas. "I saw on TV my father shaking hands with President Kennedy the morning he was killed," said New Castle resident Nancy McCauley, Evans's daughter.

Hamilton remembered he had shaken hands with Kennedy as a college student at Ball State the day before he announced his candidacy for president.

It was perhaps the first news event that highlighted the power of television, as millions were captivated by the Kennedy assassination coverage for days.

John Hodge, the veteran sports editor and occasional historical columnist at the *Courier-Times*, was a student at Test Junior High School in Richmond. "They made an announcement at the end of school that day," Hodge remembered. "You could tell that our principal, C.W. Hemmer, was emotionally affected by the news. He could barely get the words out. My family just pretty much had the TV on non-stop that whole weekend."

"The only programs on TV were about the shooting, the life of JFK and the arrest of Lee Harvey Oswald," Hamilton added. "I saw live on TV as Jack Ruby shot Oswald."

"There are a few historical events that people will always remember where they were," Hamilton continued. "For me, it is the assassination of JFK and the 9/11 terrorist attack."

Hamilton later visited the Dallas site where Kennedy was shot. While the day will forever be part of history, it also seems destined to be a day of mystery as well. "After seeing the grassy knoll and the area around it, I do not think one person could have done what Lee Harvey Oswald was charged with," Hamilton said. "It is entirely possible that Oswald was simply a scapegoat."

It's an easy day for Jennifer Thornburg Wolksi to remember, because November 22 is the day her parents got married in 1955. "I was with my mom and my younger brother in Becker Brothers grocery store," she said. "The manager came across the store intercom and announced that the President had been shot. You could have heard a pin drop. It was really eerie. What an impact on a four-year-old."

Brenda Walcott Asberry said she could relate to that sentiment. "I was almost five years old," she wrote. "I clearly remember standing in our dining room and everyone was crying. I started crying too, even though I really didn't understand what had happened."

Meanwhile, Joan Lacy Tungate was at home watching TV with her brother and sister-in-law. "We had a CB radio on in the kitchen and as

Walter Cronkite announced his death, someone came over the CB radio and played 'Taps,'" Tungate remembered. "We all got goose bumps and started crying."

Some local people were actually in Dallas when the tragedy happened. The *Courier-Times* reported that former New Castle resident Betty Poe Bradberry had watched President Kennedy and his wife pass by just seconds before the chief executive was shot. Bradberry and her husband, Jack, had been married in Dallas just two months prior to the assassination.

The assassination put a damper on regular New Castle activities. A pep parade celebrating the opening of the Trojan basketball season and a dance following the New Castle–Knightstown game were called off. The game itself was played as scheduled, with school authorities "expressing the view that the late President, an advocate of sports and physical fitness, would have wanted contracted athletic events held."

All New Castle–Henry Township schools were closed the following Monday, as were all city offices at the direction of Mayor Walter V. Falck. Only essential services of the city were performed, with even trash and garbage collections canceled.

The moment left a future New Castle speech and debate teacher speechless. "I was in study hall at the old building of Muncie Central downtown and the whole school was dismissed for the rest of the day after the announcement," said James Robbins, who, with his late wife, Joy, led many successful New Castle speech and debate contestants. "I have only felt that empty and forlorn a few times in my life."

Another future teacher, Judy Hayworth Stevens, remembers how quickly a large classroom of elementary students became library-like. "I was in Miss Sheffield's 6th-grade classroom at the old Riley School," Stevens recalled. "A mother came to pick up her son and told Miss Sheffield, but we could hear the sad news as she was delivering it. I remember all the 40-plus kids were very quiet."

Some teachers couldn't control the emotions of the moment, as Steve Guffey recalled from his Cadiz Elementary School classroom. "I was there sitting in my first grade class when the principal came over the public address system and said that the president had been shot," Guffey said. "The room fell very quiet and my teacher put her head in her hands and started sobbing uncontrollably. When she gained her composure, we all lined up to catch the bus for home early.…It was not until many years later that what happened truly set in and I realized how much America had changed on that day—Nov. 22, 1963."

Wilma Padgett, a production employee with the *Courier-Times*, stands next to a historic newspaper plate for page 1 on November 22, 1963, the day John F. Kennedy was assassinated. *From the* Courier-Times.

Wilma Padgett, who worked at the *Courier-Times* for almost fifty years, vividly recalled the day during an interview with Donna Cronk in 2015. "We watched it on TV," Wilma recalled with clarity. "The newspaper was to go to press at noon, but there was no confirmation he had died."

His death seemed a certainty, however, given that Wilma, along with most Americans, saw either live or again and again on replay the gruesome scene of the president's head being shot.

It was Wilma's job to make corrections on the linotype machine, and it was she who set the type in the story about his assassination. That typeset page remains on display at the newspaper to this day. "When confirmation finally came of the president's death, the newspaper went to press—and Wilma went to Dallas," Cronk wrote in the *Courier-Times*.

Ironically, it was her birthday, and plans were to leave with her husband for Dallas right after work to visit her brother, Lee Davis. The Padgetts waited until the next morning, and as they drove the one thousand miles, all of the radio stations were full of reports about the latest in JFK's death. The story continued to unfold as Jack Ruby shot and murdered alleged assassin Lee Harvey Oswald. In Dallas, Wilma's brother took the Padgetts on the fateful parade route.

City Editor William Crandall wrote about meeting Kennedy. It was April 12, 1959, and Senator Kennedy addressed a student assembly at Purdue University in West Lafayette that day. Crandall was a young reporter for the *Lafayette Courier and Journal* assigned to cover the senator's speech:

> *Much to my astonishment, the senator started up the steps two at a time while the official university welcoming party still was alighting from the vehicle.*
>
> *Once at the top, the senator greeted each of us with a warm smile, a handshake and a word or two. I can only say that I was greatly impressed by his warm friendliness and his mental and physical vigor.*

As Sen. Kennedy entered the administration building, I couldn't help notice with some humor that the official welcoming party was still climbing up the steps in a desperate attempt to catch up.

That day the senator told the students "our country needs strong citizens and leadership as well as weapons" and he was greeted by a standing ovation.

In closing his talk that spring day, Sen. Kennedy said "as we face the dark future, we must bring candles to illuminate our country's way."

Sulphur Springs Gas Pipeline Explosion Seared into the Memory of Henry County Residents

Was it a plane crash? Did one of New Castle's steel mills or an area silo explode? An Indianapolis Associated Press editor feared, since the fireball was seen in the east, that Washington, D.C., had been attacked. A few faithful Christian believers wondered if the brightness in the sky meant that the rapture was at hand and Jesus Christ had returned.

During the early evening hours of November 23, 1993, the tiny town of Sulphur Springs found itself the center of major media attention. A massive explosion cast a bright-orange glow seen as far away as Lafayette, Fort Wayne, Indianapolis, and Louisville, Kentucky. It was an event that put Sulphur Springs on the map. Three decades later, people are grateful that it didn't blow the small town off that map at the same time.

A recent Facebook post by the Henry County Historical Society generated quite the response concerning memories of the event.

Delora Hartsock and Franki Zile, *Courier-Times* reporters at the time, wrote that investigators concluded drainage work being done in a field near Sulphur Springs had damaged a gas pipeline, causing it to weaken over a two-week period and eventually explode. The power of that explosion was immense. "The ground around it looks like a volcano," one law enforcement officer said at the scene.

John McCormack said that some of his neighbors had windows shattered due to the force of the explosion. As Carolyn Ford Utt drove up her lane, she thought that their hog barn was on fire. Jen Hank wondered if a crop duster known to fly in that area had crashed.

Some reports estimated flames from the explosion to be a mile high. "I could see it from 10th and Shadeland in Indianapolis," Alice Toole said.

"I was driving back from Bloomington and could see it down around Martinsville," Dave Rodecap remembered.

Those who remember the event also recall the sounds as well as the sights. It reminded some of a rocket-like propulsion as the fire continued to burn, almost as if a Space Shuttle had launched in a Sulphur Springs farm field. "The glow made it look like an orange daylight and the vibrating roar sound lasted for hours," Teresa Miller Umbarger said.

Bill Ward, a Henry County sheriff's deputy at the time, thought that a jet from Grissom Air Force Base might have crashed. "Whatever had happened, it was something providing the fire with plenty of fuel," Ward remembered.

Complicating efforts to respond were hundreds of sightseers driving toward the orange glow. "Many first responders couldn't get near the area due to traffic backups," Ward remembered. "It really didn't matter because there was really nothing anyone could do. Eventually, as the fire got smaller and smaller, the traffic slowly disappeared."

Charles Blaydes remembered that local law enforcement officials handled the difficult situation well. "You did exactly what common sense would tell you to do," Blaydes said. "Set up a perimeter and letting the fire burn itself out is all that anyone could do."

Middletown's Marty Ballard was leading a girls' basketball team practice when the explosion occurred. "Rachel Russell shot a three-pointer that hit the rim—and the lights went out," Ballard remembered. "She screamed 'it wasn't me!' We went outside and thought a plane had crashed. Practice was over."

Miraculously, no one was hurt. Marcia Shock remembers her young child's precious reaction just like it was yesterday. "We were at Scatterfield waiting to turn east onto 53rd Street," she posted on Facebook. "Seeing the bright light of the explosion, my young child leaned up and said 'is it Jesus coming back?' Good response. Ready for the rapture? I thought he was right."

Henry County Tornados

Two terrifying tornados, fifty-seven years apart, are remembered in Henry County for the deaths and destruction they caused. Yet, at the same time, they are also bound together in the annals of history by inspiration that rose above the rubble, first in New Castle on March 11, 1917, and then on April 3, 1974, in Kennard.

New Castle Tornado

It was a Sunday afternoon when a loud, freight train–like noise got the attention of Harry Cottrell's mother in New Castle.

"Was that the Cincinnati Express passing?" Cottrell's mother asked.

"Oh no," Cottrell, an avid train watcher, told his mom. "That went by a half an hour ago."

What they heard was no freight train. It was a massive tornado. At 3:02 p.m. on Sunday, March 11, 1917, many New Castle lives were changed forever. In just a few terrifying minutes, twenty-two people were killed, hundreds were injured, five hundred homes were damaged or destroyed and many of the city's triumphant greenhouses were leveled in what would be part of $1 million suffered in property damage. Today, that would translate to more than $24 million.

"Men, women and children are seen on every hand with arms in slings, bandages around heads and liberal patches on faces," a New Castle newspaper read. "The two morgues were filled with a never-ending stream of visitors from daylight until late in the evening. It was estimated that 10,000 or more viewed the remains of victims in the disaster. Tear-stained eyes of many visitors indicated that they had friends among the dead, but the majority of the visitors were attracted to the city only from curiosity."

The tragedy, which still ranks as one of the worst tornado disasters in Indiana history, defied a once-held scientific belief that a twister of that magnitude would never hit New Castle. For years and years, men of science were emphatic in their declaration that a cyclone could not hit New Castle," an *Indianapolis Star* article noted. "They based their assertion on the location of New Castle, it being situated on elevated ground with a wide valley lying between the town and a higher elevation on the west."

And yet, looks of stunned disbelief were captured in many photographs after the storm. That included three men standing amid the rubble of what used to be one of New Castle's one hundred greenhouses. The city was once known as the "Rose City," but after the devastation, greenhouses would never again come close to their peak sales of flowers.

There were miracles in the midst of the madness, however. The *Courier* reported that a baby of Mr. and Mrs. Charles Albert was upstairs asleep. As the storm passed, Mrs. Albert ran upstairs. All of the roof had been blown away from the house except for the roof above the baby's head. "The noise of the tornado and crashing timbers, however, did not awaken the baby, which slept on," the newspaper reported.

A clean-up worker takes a break following the March 11, 1917 tornado that hit New Castle, Indiana. *From the* Courier-Times.

Another incident reported that three-year-old Ruth Fletcher was picked up by the tornado at 25th Street and Grand Avenue and then dropped in a vacant lot. The child's cries attracted a rescuer, who took her to a physician's office.

The *Courier* reported that Ida Lawson, who was living at 1211 Lincoln Avenue, had just left the home headed to town. She was unable to return to the house and grabbed a small cedar tree. "The tree she had chosen was the only one on Lincoln Avenue that had remained standing. A much larger tree in the yard east of her was blown over, and if she had been holding to it, she would have met certain death," the newspaper reported.

New Castle had two newspapers at the time, the *Courier* and the *Times*. The two wouldn't officially merge until 1930, but the first issue of the *Courier-Times* was actually published the day after the deadly tornado.

On Monday, March 12, 1917, the city was busy burying the dead, caring for the injured, reclaiming property—too busy recovering for the staffs of the *Courier* and the *Times* to work full time putting out two newspapers. So the first *Courier-Times* appeared that Monday morning with an extra and again in the evening with another extra.

Kennard Tornado

A little more than fifty-seven years later, it was a sunny morning in the small town of Kennard, located just over seven miles west of New

Castle. Teacher Janet Sparks remembered her students played a game of kickball in the sunshine. Then, suddenly, dark clouds rolled in and the temperature dropped.

Ironically—or by the grace of God—students had their very first tornado drill just the day before. "Our stately edifice was approaching 100 years old," Janet said. "First and second grade students were placed in coat closets that stretched across the back of their classrooms. The remaining grades were strategically placed in the basement. Our principal, Mr. Donald Newcomer, walked up and down the stairs checking the placement of the classes. After the practice, I returned to my classroom not thinking about a storm and the need for this drill."

But as teacher Jackie Harris remembered on that fateful April 3, "It just kept getting darker and darker." The rain began to pound against the building. The time on the clock was 3:00 p.m. Shirley Sheppard, a teacher aide at that time and later Kennard secretary, remembered the expression Principal Newcomer had on his face when the phone rang as school was dismissing. Students were already boarding when she said Newcomer just threw the phone down and went straight to the school buses.

Cars were tossed around like toys during the April 3, 1974 tornado that hit Kennard, Indiana. *From the* Courier-Times.

With the remains of the Kennard school in the background, U.S. Senator Birch Bayh surveys the tornado damage with a local resident after the April 3, 1974 tornado that decimated the small Henry County town. *From the* Courier-Times.

"He ran out the door toward the two buses and took the kids off, telling them to run to the building," Janet Sparks said. "I had never seen it rain so hard. The students were soaked when they entered the building. Teachers escorted students to their 'safe places.'"

Shirley Sheppard remembered Glenna Womack, a friend who had been cleaning the nearby Kennard church, running into the school screaming, "It's coming! It's coming!" "She no sooner said that when the lights went out," Sheppard said.

"I placed myself like the children on the floor of the basement and said a prayer," Janet Sparks said. "I remember the great pressure in my ears as objects, papers and debris flew around my head. As quickly as the tornado began, it was over. I asked my fourth graders if they were all right. Not one had a physical complaint. Several students had tears in their eyes and all of them were skittish, the same as me."

The freight train roar above them was something many teachers said they would never forget. That frightening sound was matched by the equally intense silence of the children. Teacher Helen Dulin recalled that the kids were relatively calm and quiet throughout it all. "They hovered close to you," she said. "They really didn't cry. I felt like a hen with a bunch of young chicks."

"Mr. Newcomer once again made the rounds, checking on the students' well-being," Janet Sparks said, describing the aftermath of the storm. "To my knowledge, there were no injuries in the basement. Parents began entering the battered building to claim their kids, yelling with sighs of relief as they hugged their children.

"Without the tornado drill, the strategical placement of the classes and the calm thinking of Mr. Newcomer, the outcome for Kennard students and staff on April 3, 1974, would have been much different. Mr. Don Newcomer is my school hero."

About the Author

A lifelong resident of Henry County, Darrel Radford has been a journalist since his senior year at Blue River Valley High School nearly fifty years ago. With experience in newspapers, radio, magazines and politics, Radford says that he's never met a story assignment he didn't like. Author or coauthor of five books, Radford has had leadership roles on newspaper staffs in New Castle, Knightstown, Winchester and Hartford City and received numerous awards for his work. He continues to life in the New Castle area with his wife, Becky. They are parents of two children, Molly and Derek, as well as two grandchildren, Claire and Hallie.

Visit us at
www.historypress.com